PUCKER

The Seductive Art of MATT BUSCH

AF587908

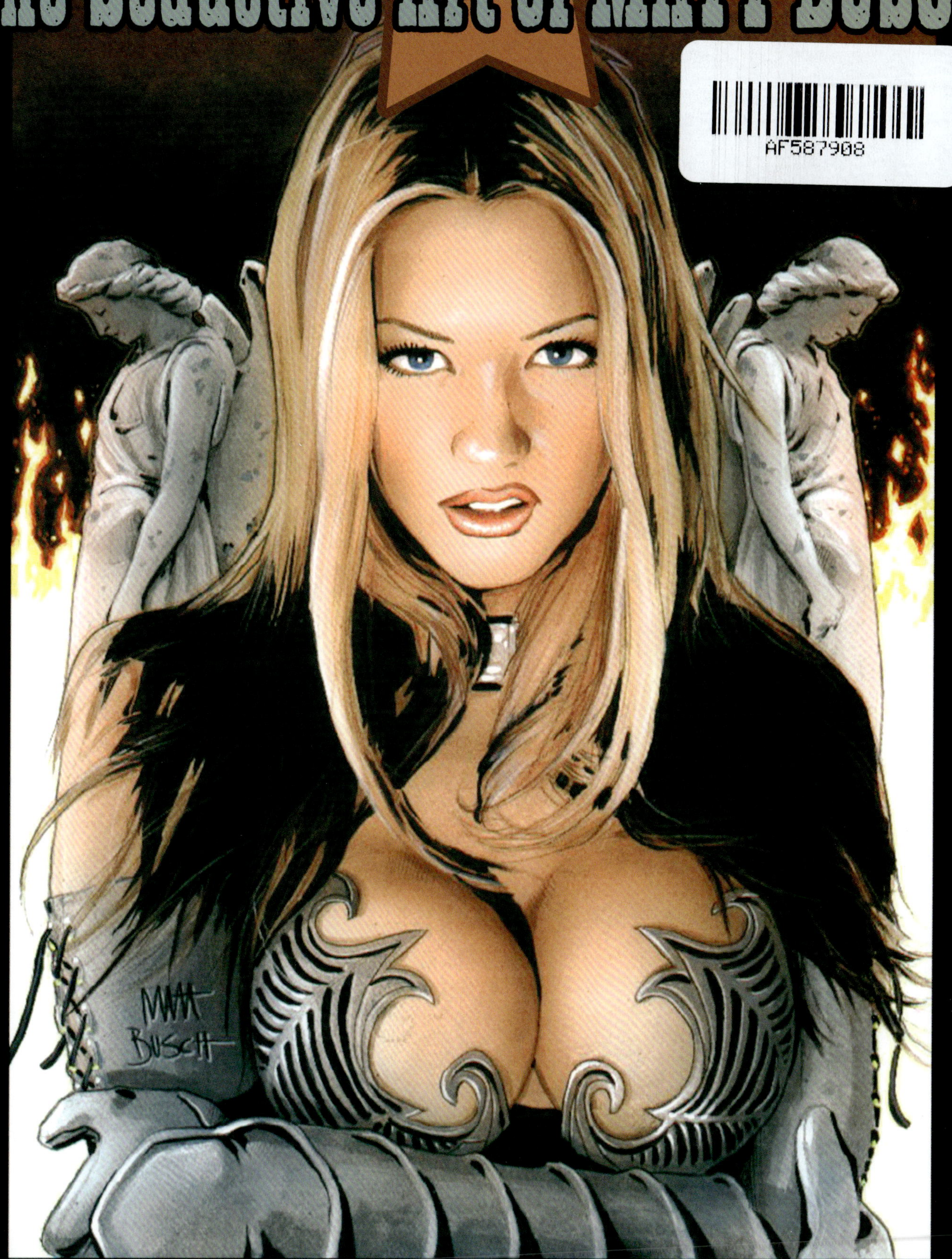

An SQP Presentation

ABOUT THE ARTIST

"Providing Junk Food to the Art World since 1972"

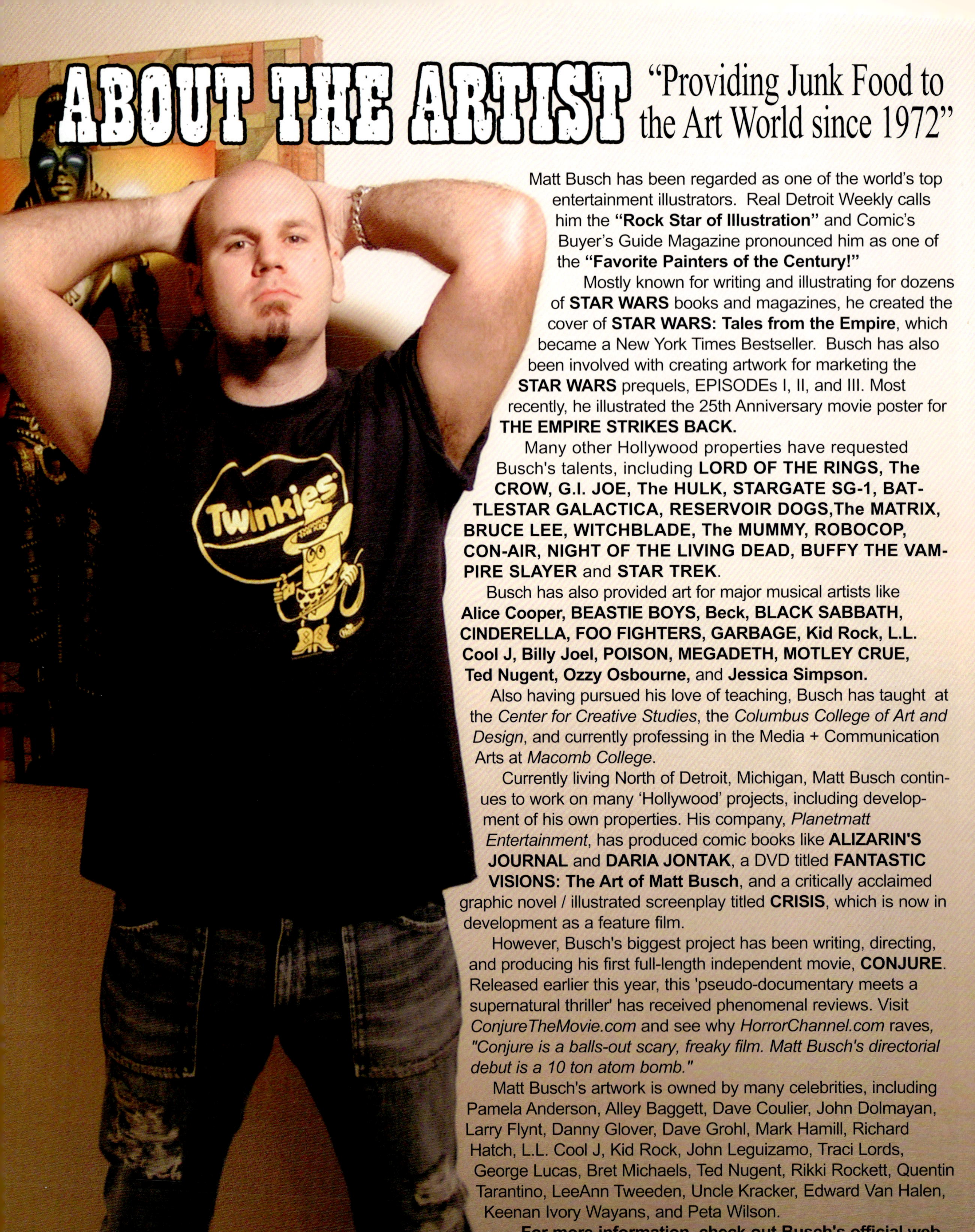

Matt Busch has been regarded as one of the world's top entertainment illustrators. Real Detroit Weekly calls him the **"Rock Star of Illustration"** and Comic's Buyer's Guide Magazine pronounced him as one of the **"Favorite Painters of the Century!"**

Mostly known for writing and illustrating for dozens of **STAR WARS** books and magazines, he created the cover of **STAR WARS: Tales from the Empire**, which became a New York Times Bestseller. Busch has also been involved with creating artwork for marketing the **STAR WARS** prequels, EPISODEs I, II, and III. Most recently, he illustrated the 25th Anniversary movie poster for **THE EMPIRE STRIKES BACK.**

Many other Hollywood properties have requested Busch's talents, including **LORD OF THE RINGS, The CROW, G.I. JOE, The HULK, STARGATE SG-1, BATTLESTAR GALACTICA, RESERVOIR DOGS,The MATRIX, BRUCE LEE, WITCHBLADE, The MUMMY, ROBOCOP, CON-AIR, NIGHT OF THE LIVING DEAD, BUFFY THE VAMPIRE SLAYER** and **STAR TREK**.

Busch has also provided art for major musical artists like **Alice Cooper, BEASTIE BOYS, Beck, BLACK SABBATH, CINDERELLA, FOO FIGHTERS, GARBAGE, Kid Rock, L.L. Cool J, Billy Joel, POISON, MEGADETH, MOTLEY CRUE, Ted Nugent, Ozzy Osbourne,** and **Jessica Simpson.**

Also having pursued his love of teaching, Busch has taught at the *Center for Creative Studies*, the *Columbus College of Art and Design*, and currently professing in the Media + Communication Arts at *Macomb College*.

Currently living North of Detroit, Michigan, Matt Busch continues to work on many 'Hollywood' projects, including development of his own properties. His company, *Planetmatt Entertainment*, has produced comic books like **ALIZARIN'S JOURNAL** and **DARIA JONTAK**, a DVD titled **FANTASTIC VISIONS: The Art of Matt Busch**, and a critically acclaimed graphic novel / illustrated screenplay titled **CRISIS**, which is now in development as a feature film.

However, Busch's biggest project has been writing, directing, and producing his first full-length independent movie, **CONJURE**. Released earlier this year, this 'pseudo-documentary meets a supernatural thriller' has received phenomenal reviews. Visit *ConjureTheMovie.com* and see why *HorrorChannel.com* raves, *"Conjure is a balls-out scary, freaky film. Matt Busch's directorial debut is a 10 ton atom bomb."*

Matt Busch's artwork is owned by many celebrities, including Pamela Anderson, Alley Baggett, Dave Coulier, John Dolmayan, Larry Flynt, Danny Glover, Dave Grohl, Mark Hamill, Richard Hatch, L.L. Cool J, Kid Rock, John Leguizamo, Traci Lords, George Lucas, Bret Michaels, Ted Nugent, Rikki Rockett, Quentin Tarantino, LeeAnn Tweeden, Uncle Kracker, Edward Van Halen, Keenan Ivory Wayans, and Peta Wilson.

For more information, check out Busch's official web site, MattBusch.com.

Pucker: The Seductive Art of Matt Busch - All artwork is copyright © 2006 Matt Busch. All characters are copyright © their respective owners.
Pucker: The Seductive Art of Matt Busch is copyright © 2006 S.Q. Productions Inc. All rights reserved. Printed in China.
Publishers Sal Quartuccio and Bob Keenan. SQP Inc - PO Box 248 - Columbus, NJ 08022. Send for our free full color catalog - www.sqpinc.com

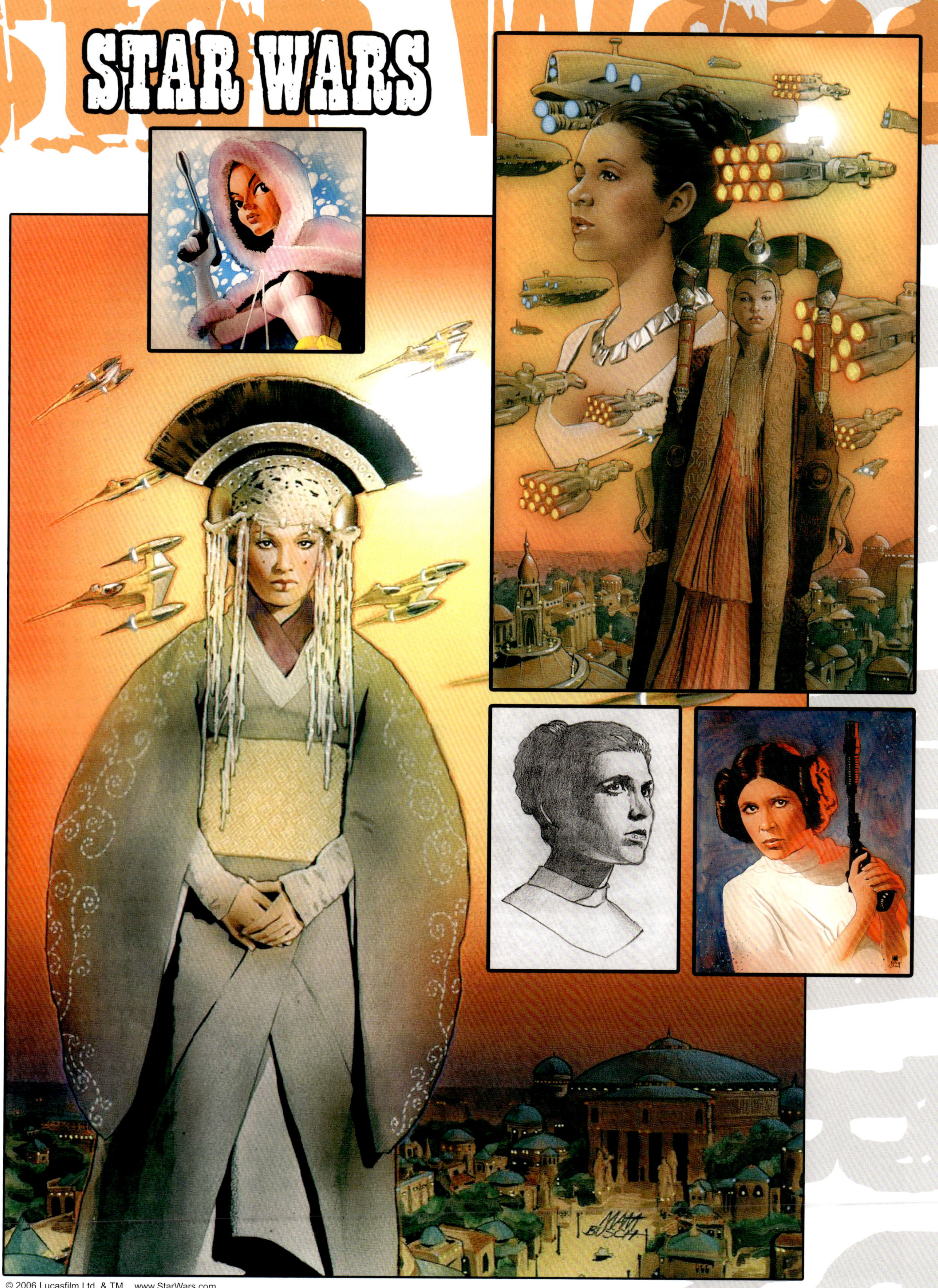

© 2006 Lucasfilm Ltd. & TM. www.StarWars.com

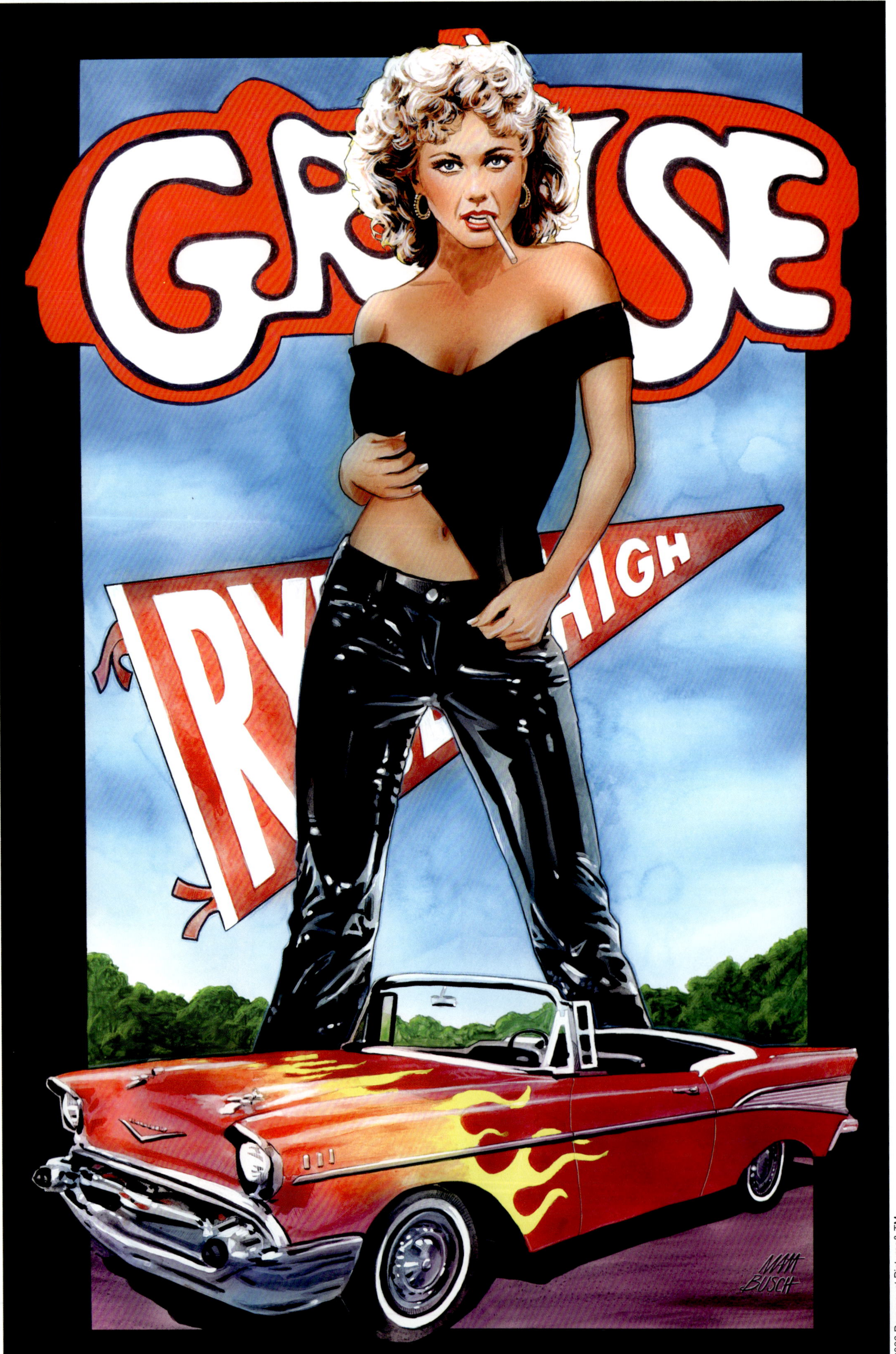

© 2006 Paramount Pictures& TM

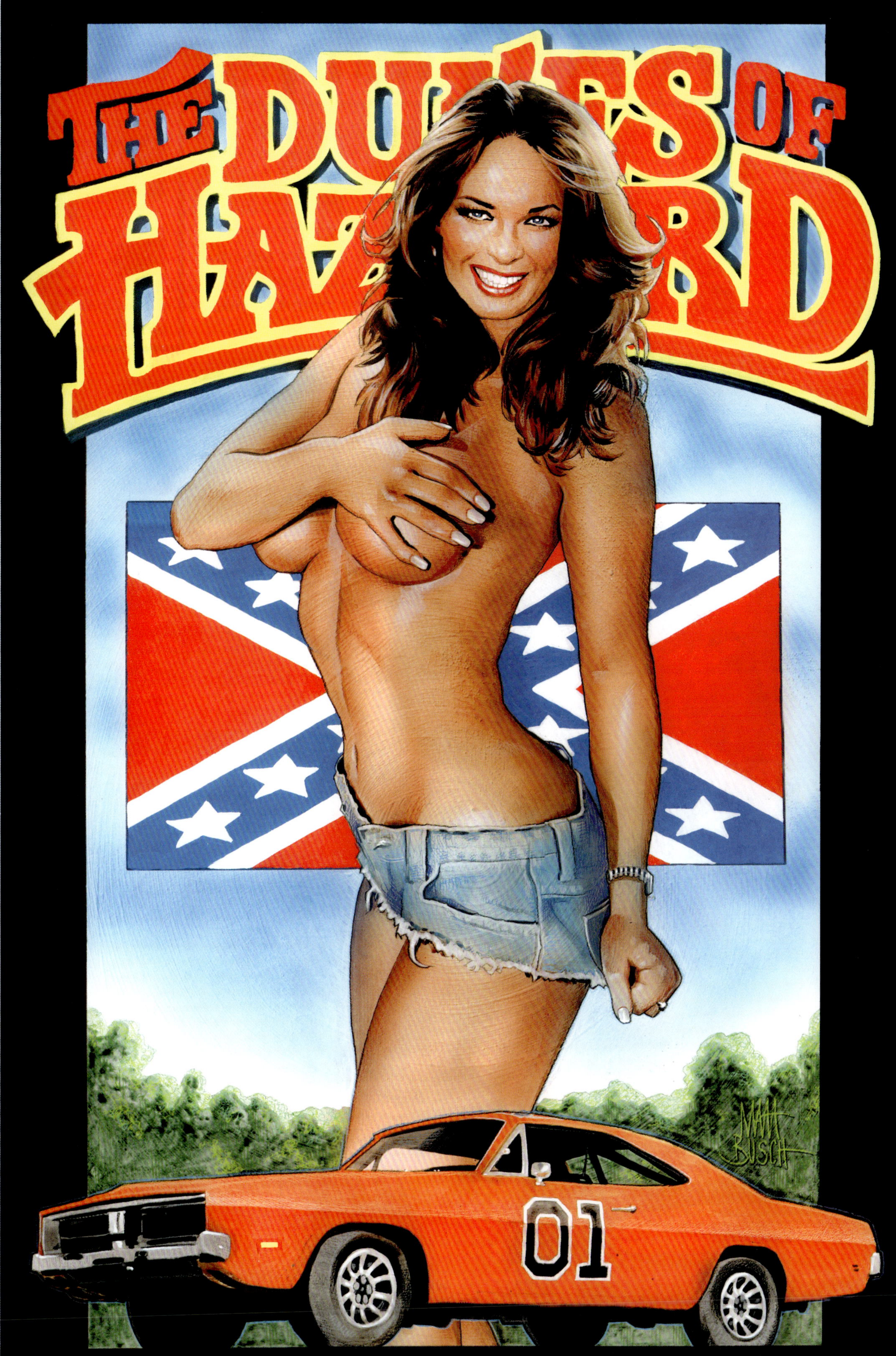

© 2006 Warner Bros. Entertainment Inc. & TM

ALLEY BAGGETT

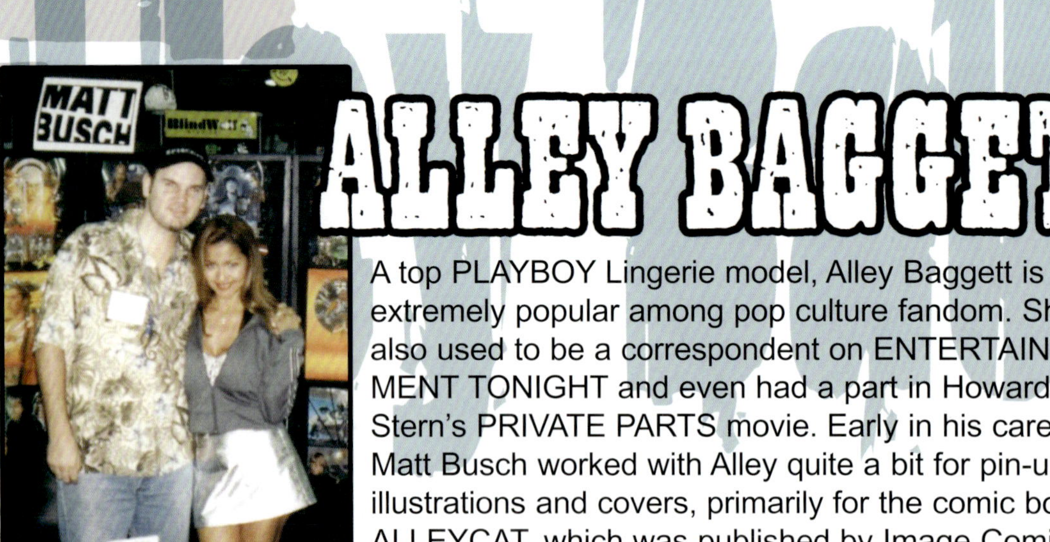

A top PLAYBOY Lingerie model, Alley Baggett is extremely popular among pop culture fandom. She also used to be a correspondent on ENTERTAINMENT TONIGHT and even had a part in Howard Stern's PRIVATE PARTS movie. Early in his career, Matt Busch worked with Alley quite a bit for pin-up illustrations and covers, primarily for the comic book ALLEYCAT, which was published by Image Comics.

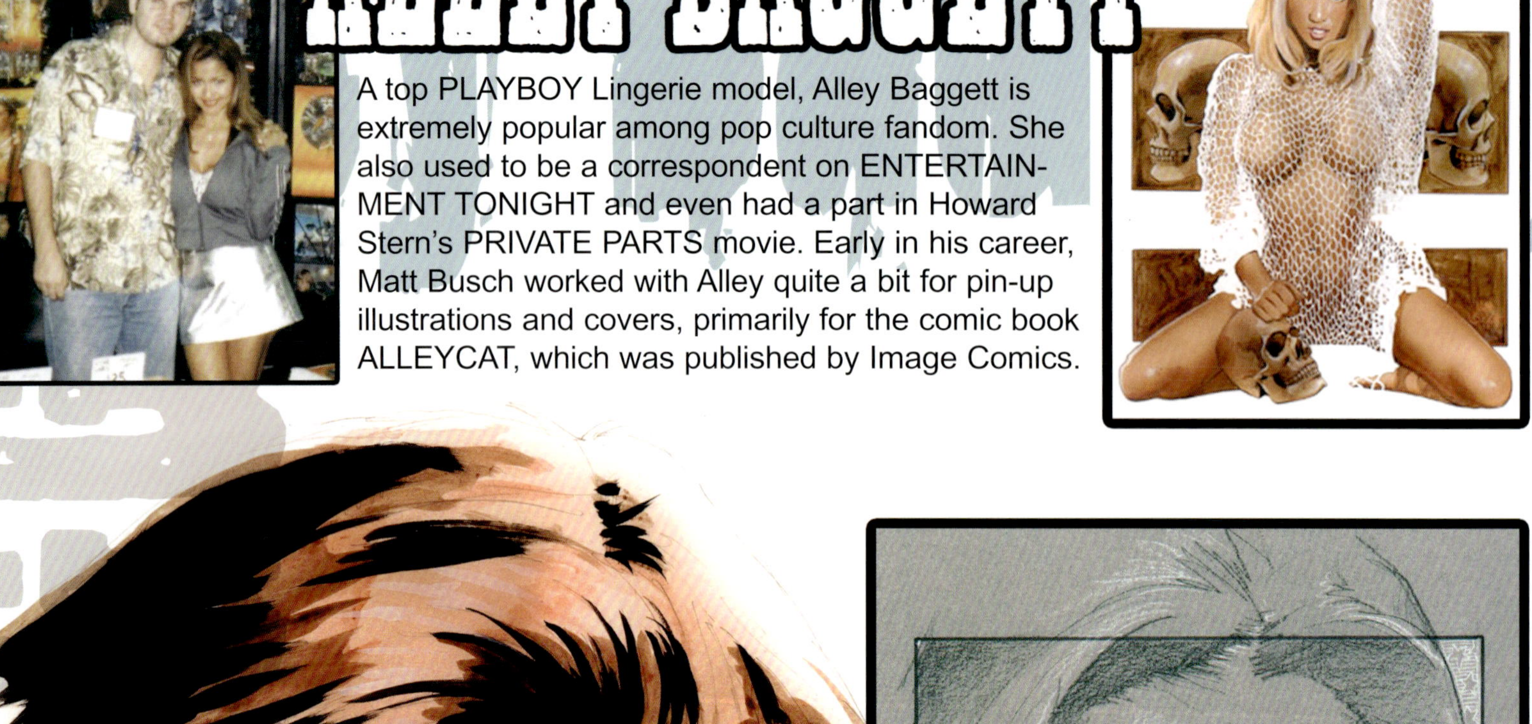

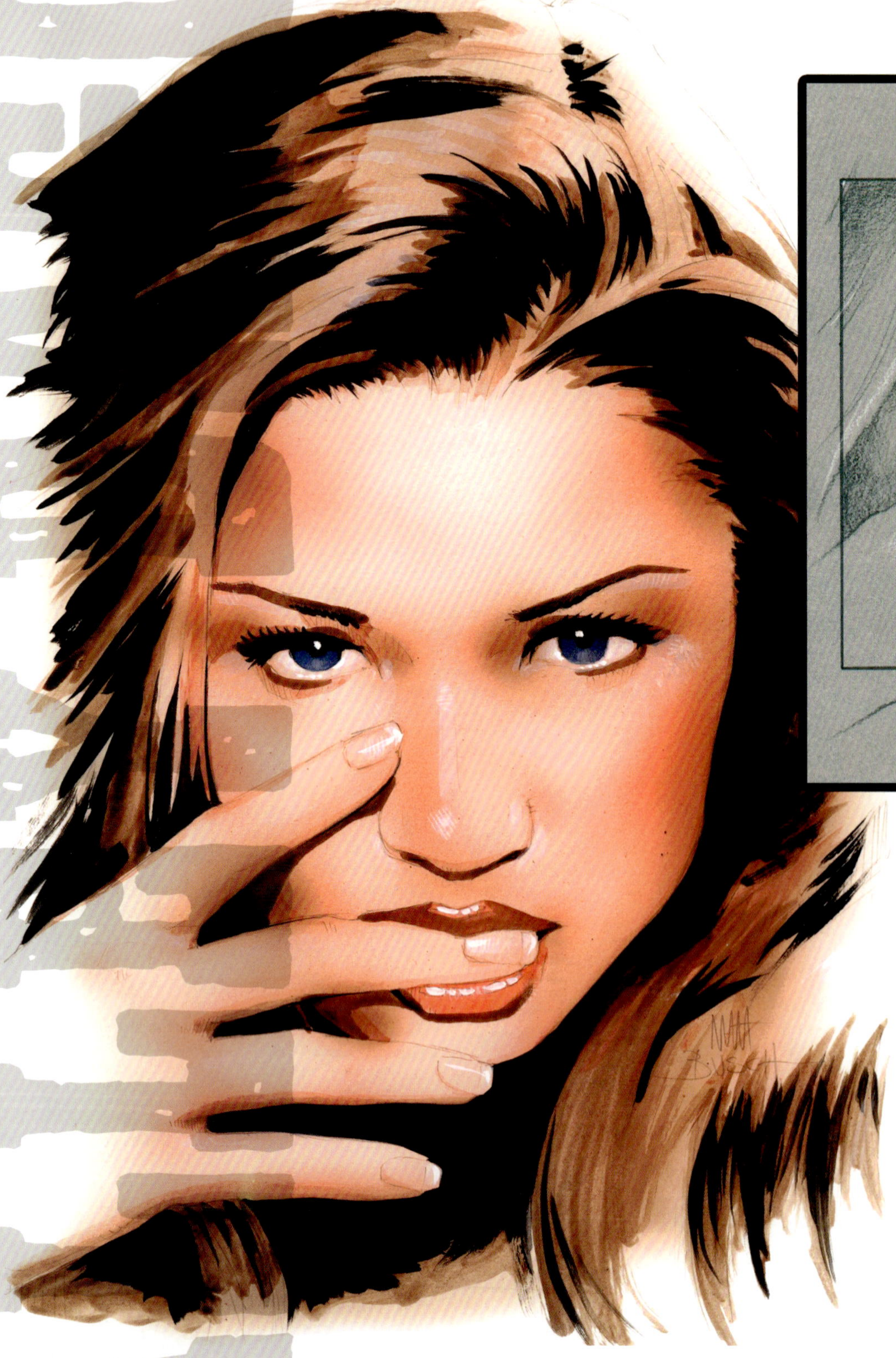

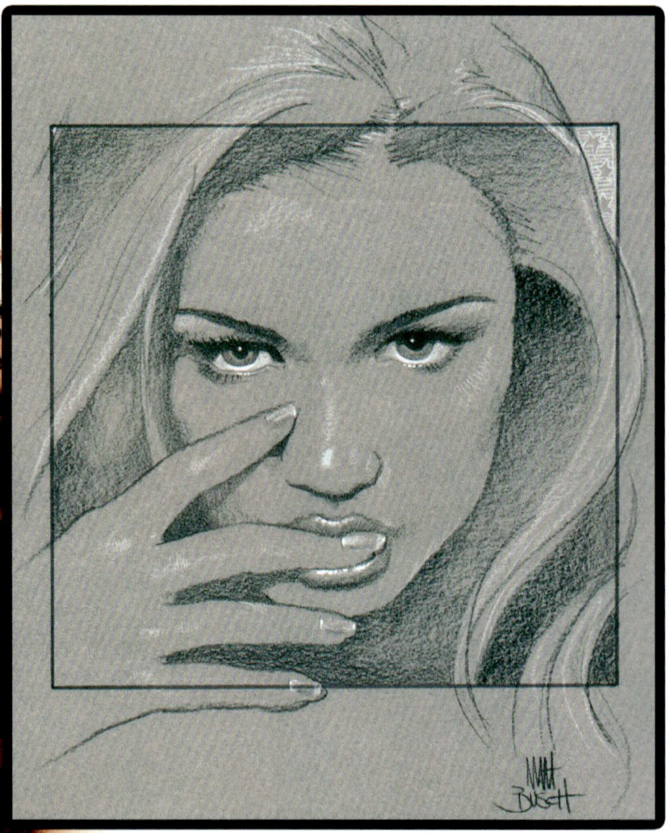

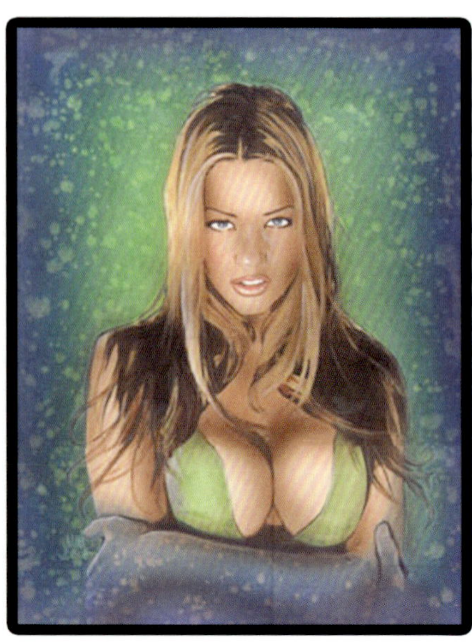

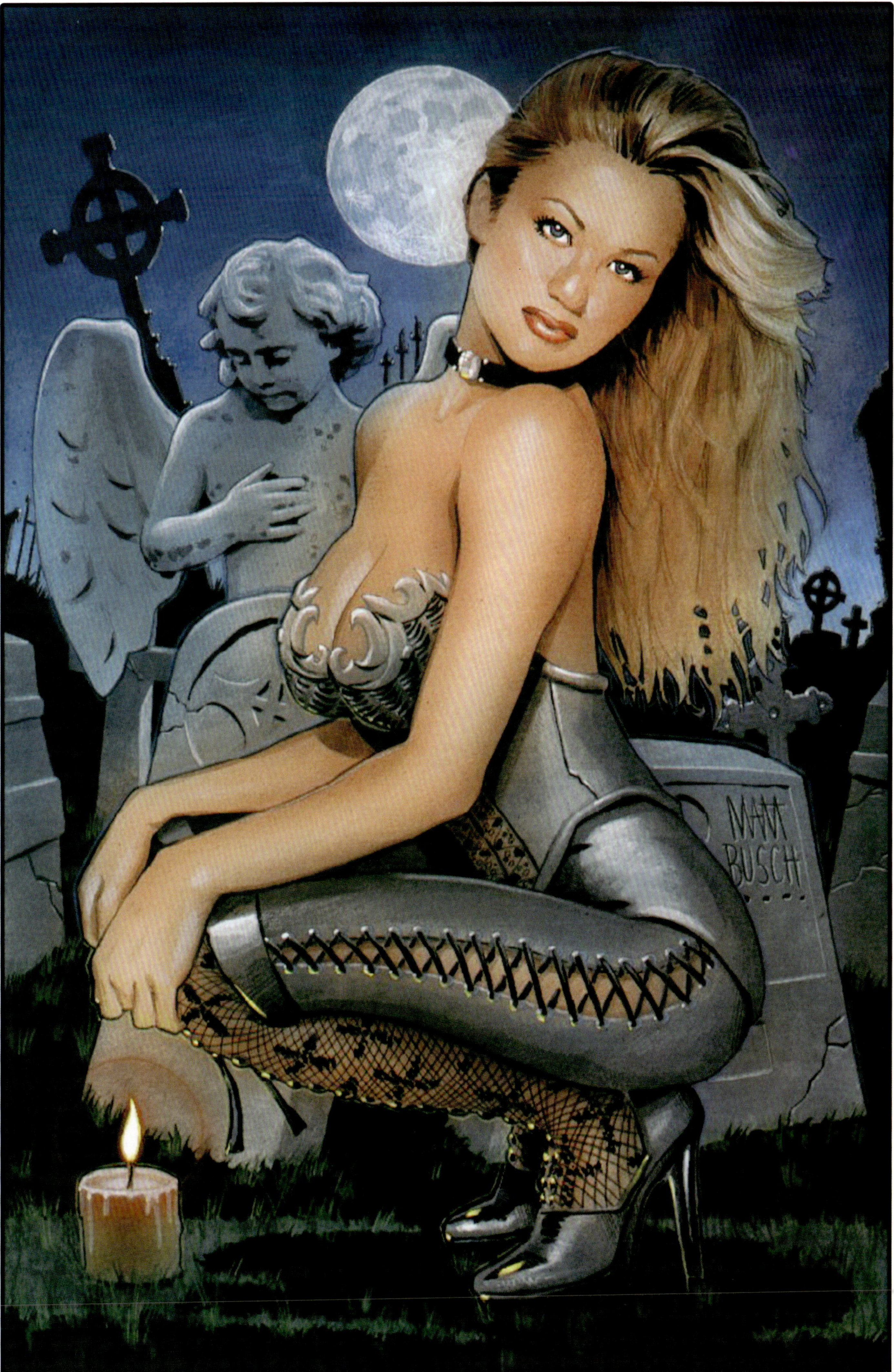
MATT BUSCH

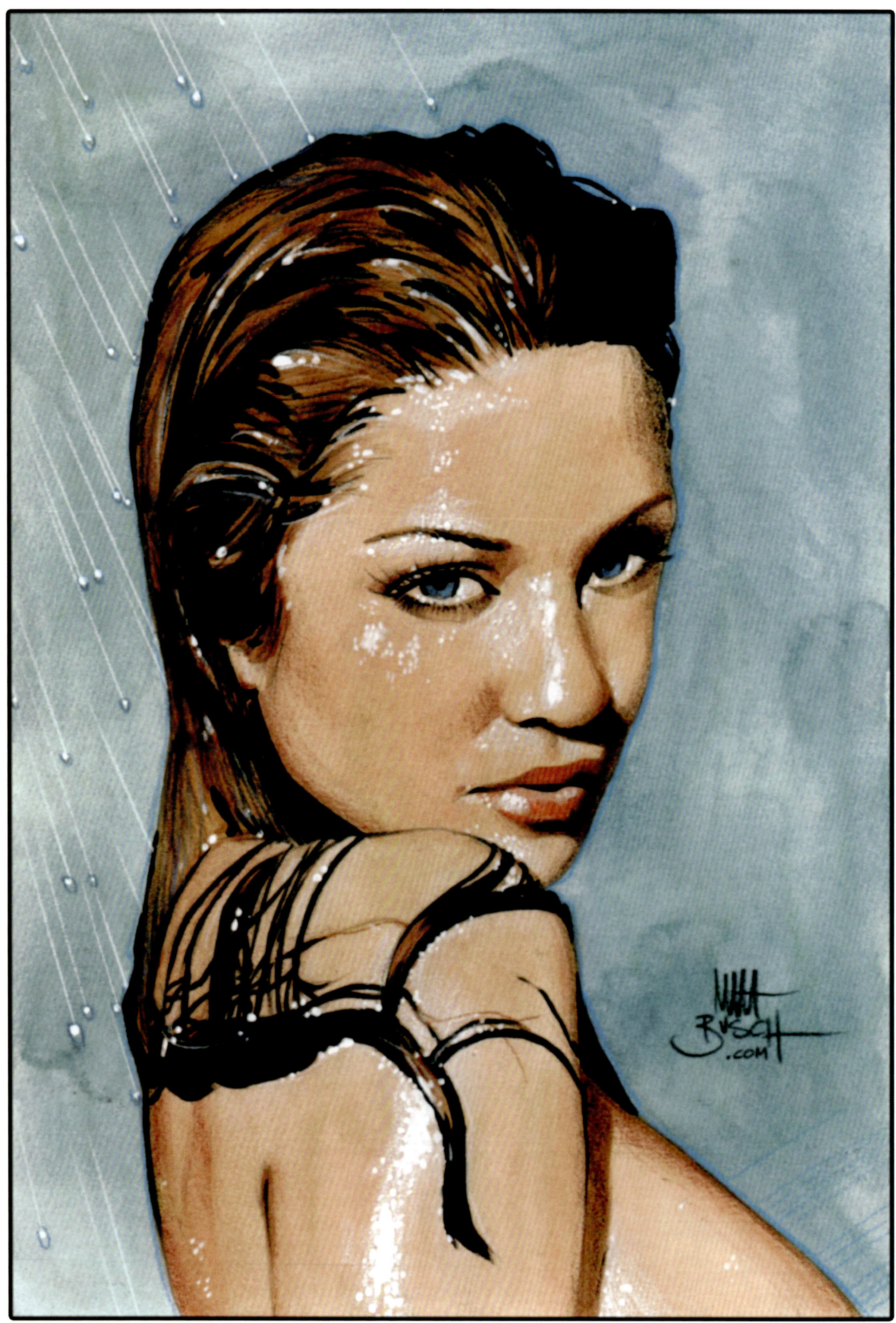

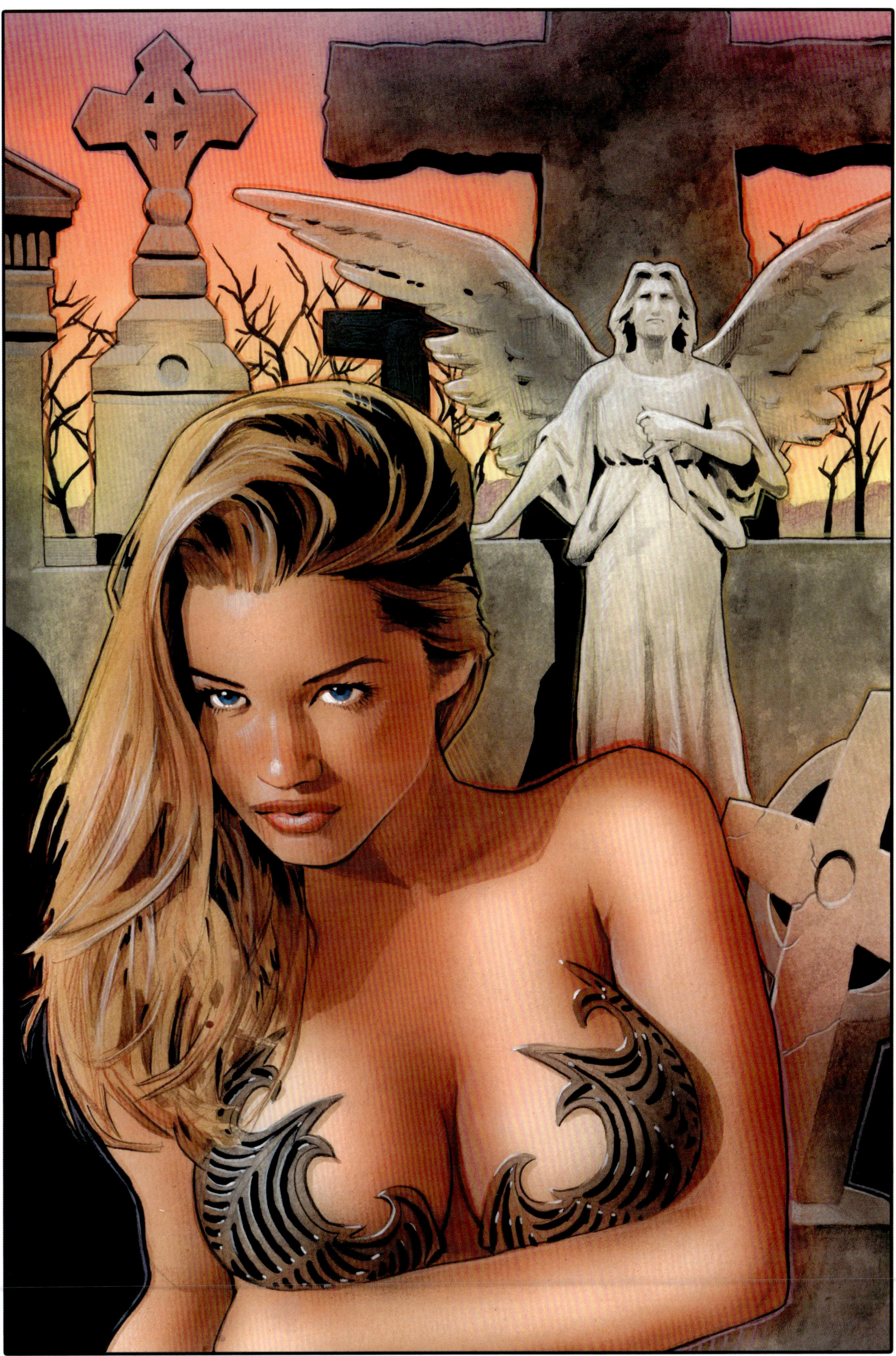

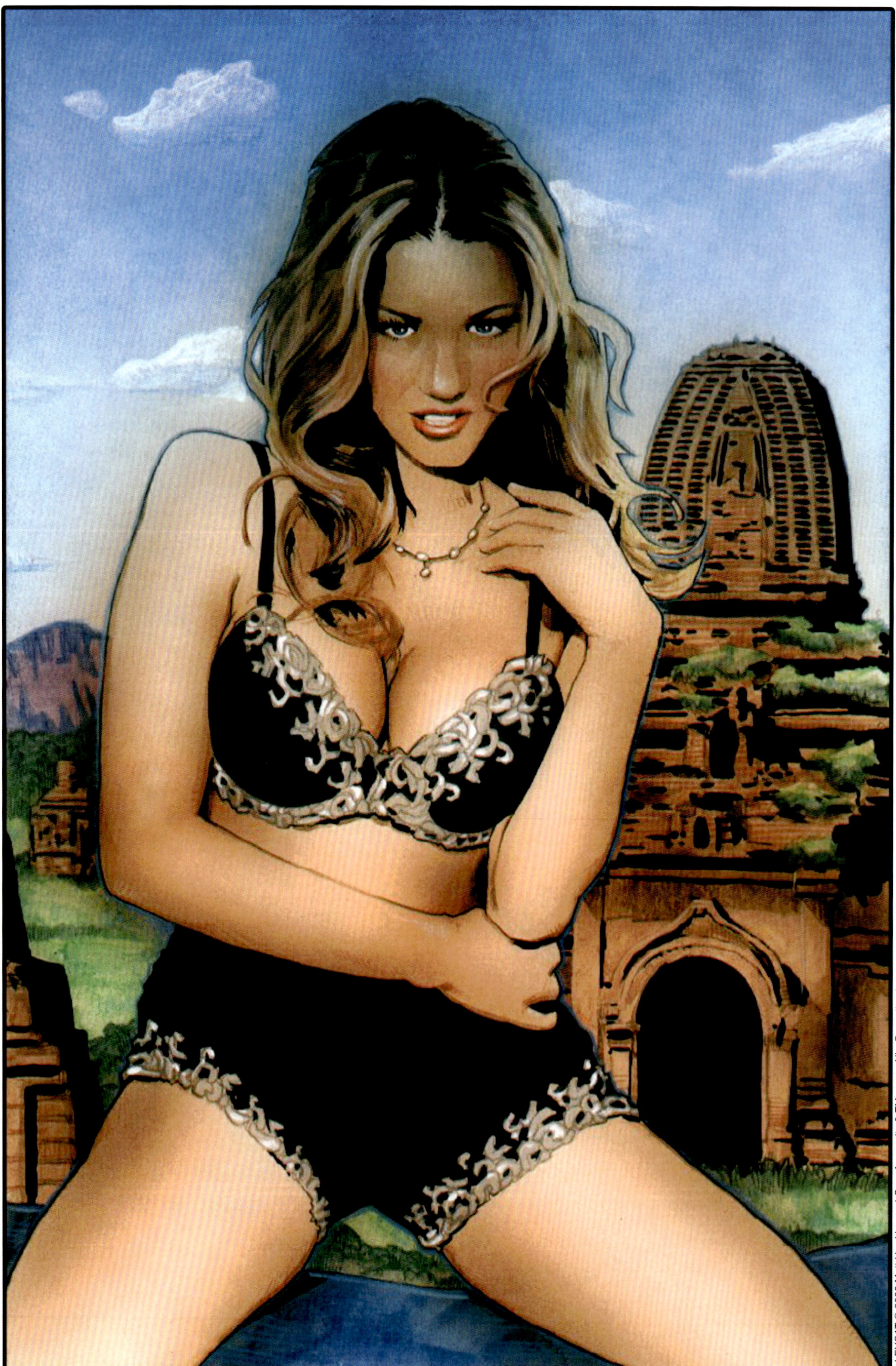

ALLEYCAT © 2006 Matt Hawkins and Greg Aronowitz & TM. www.AlleyBaggett.net

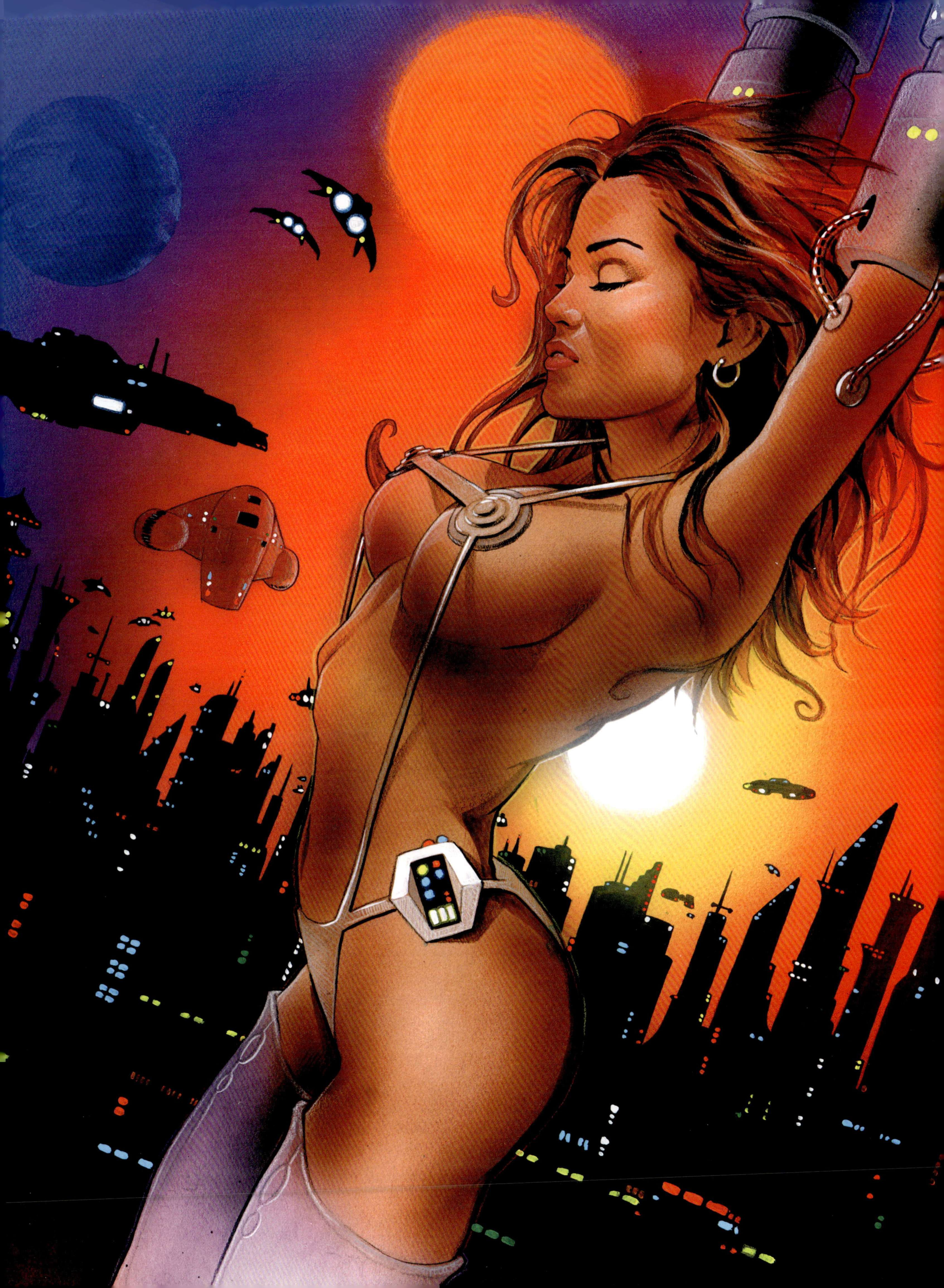

DARIA JONTAK

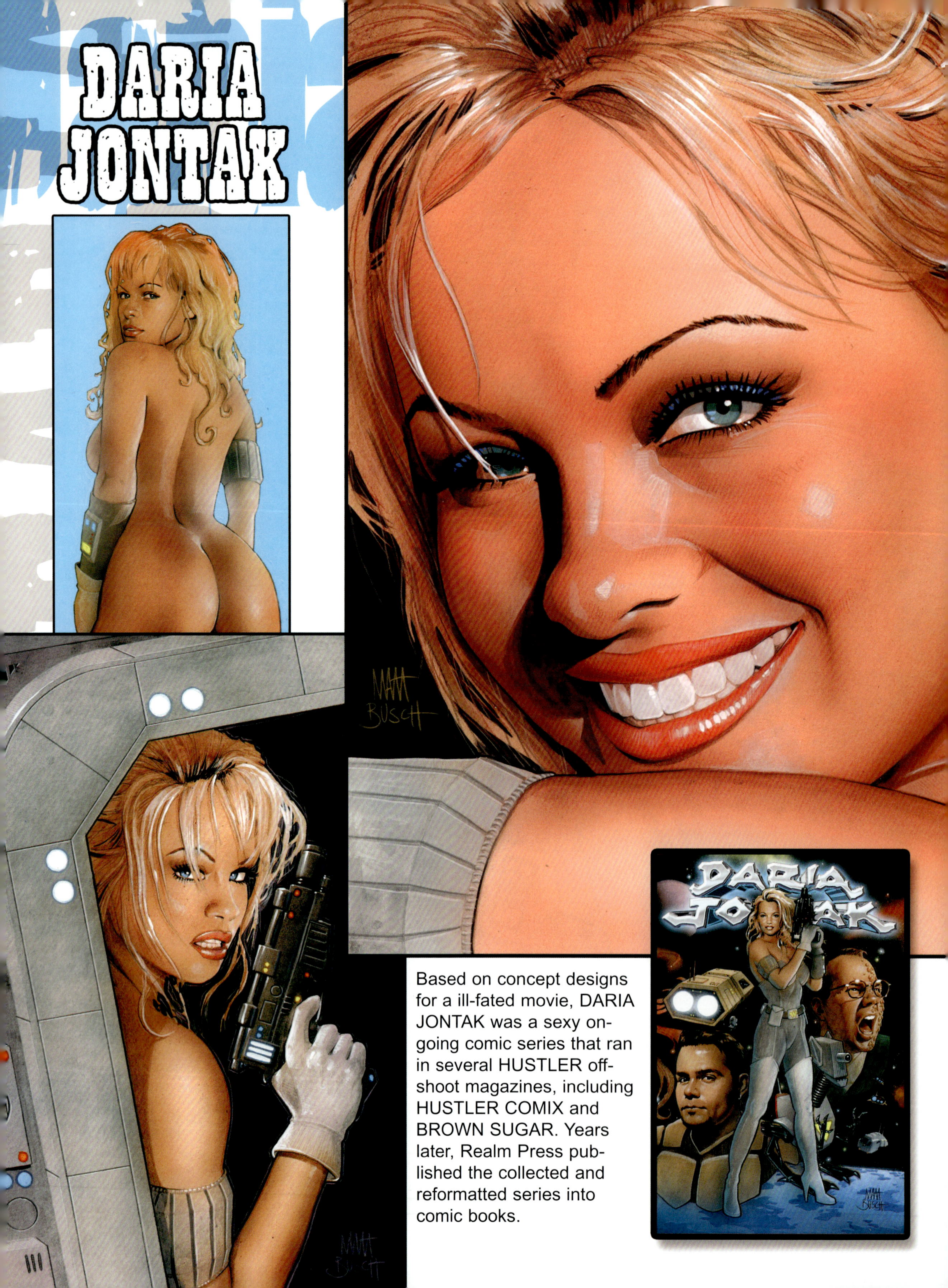

Based on concept designs for a ill-fated movie, DARIA JONTAK was a sexy on-going comic series that ran in several HUSTLER off-shoot magazines, including HUSTLER COMIX and BROWN SUGAR. Years later, Realm Press published the collected and reformatted series into comic books.

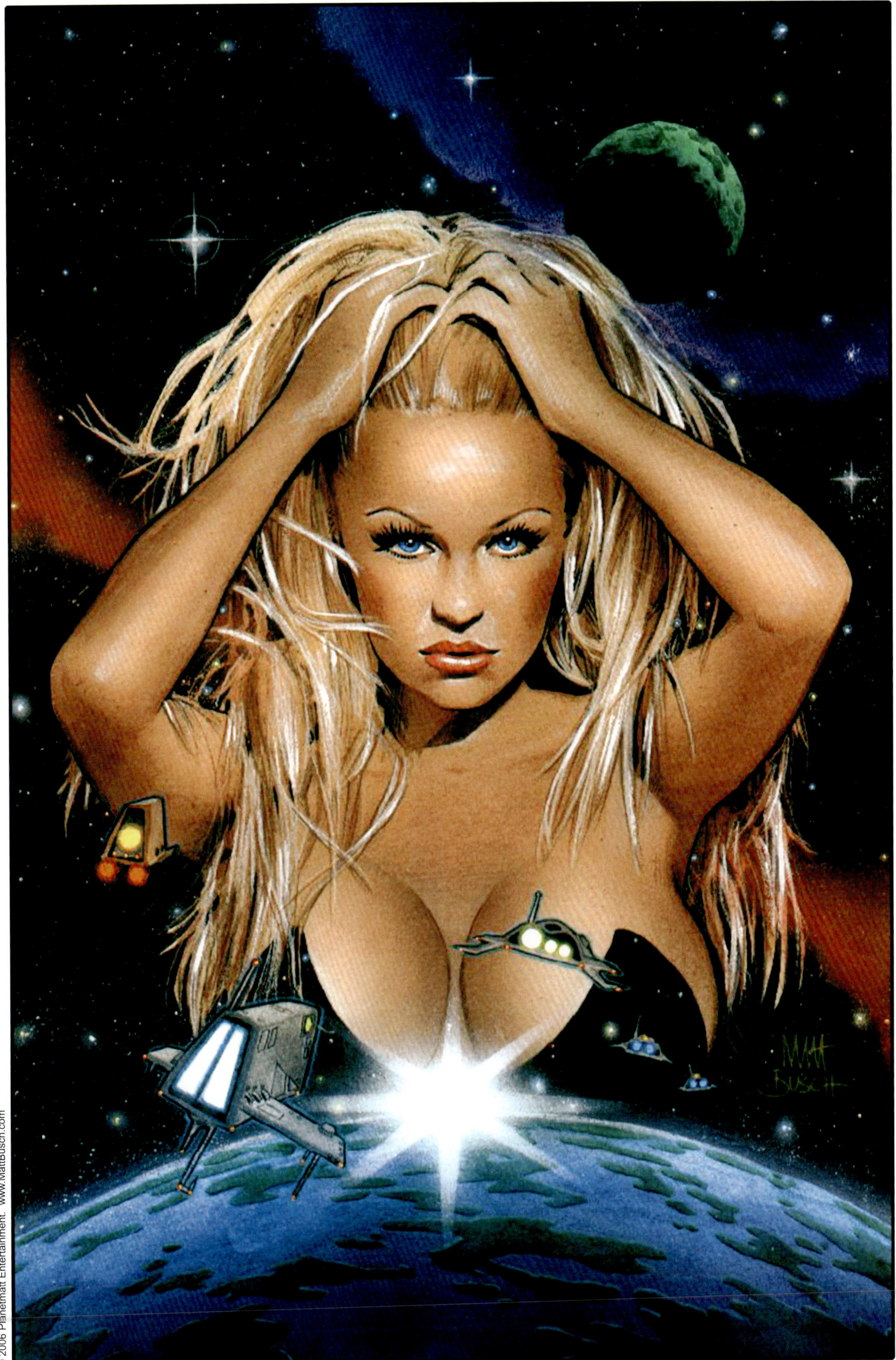

© 2006 Planetmatt Entertainment. www.MattBusch.com

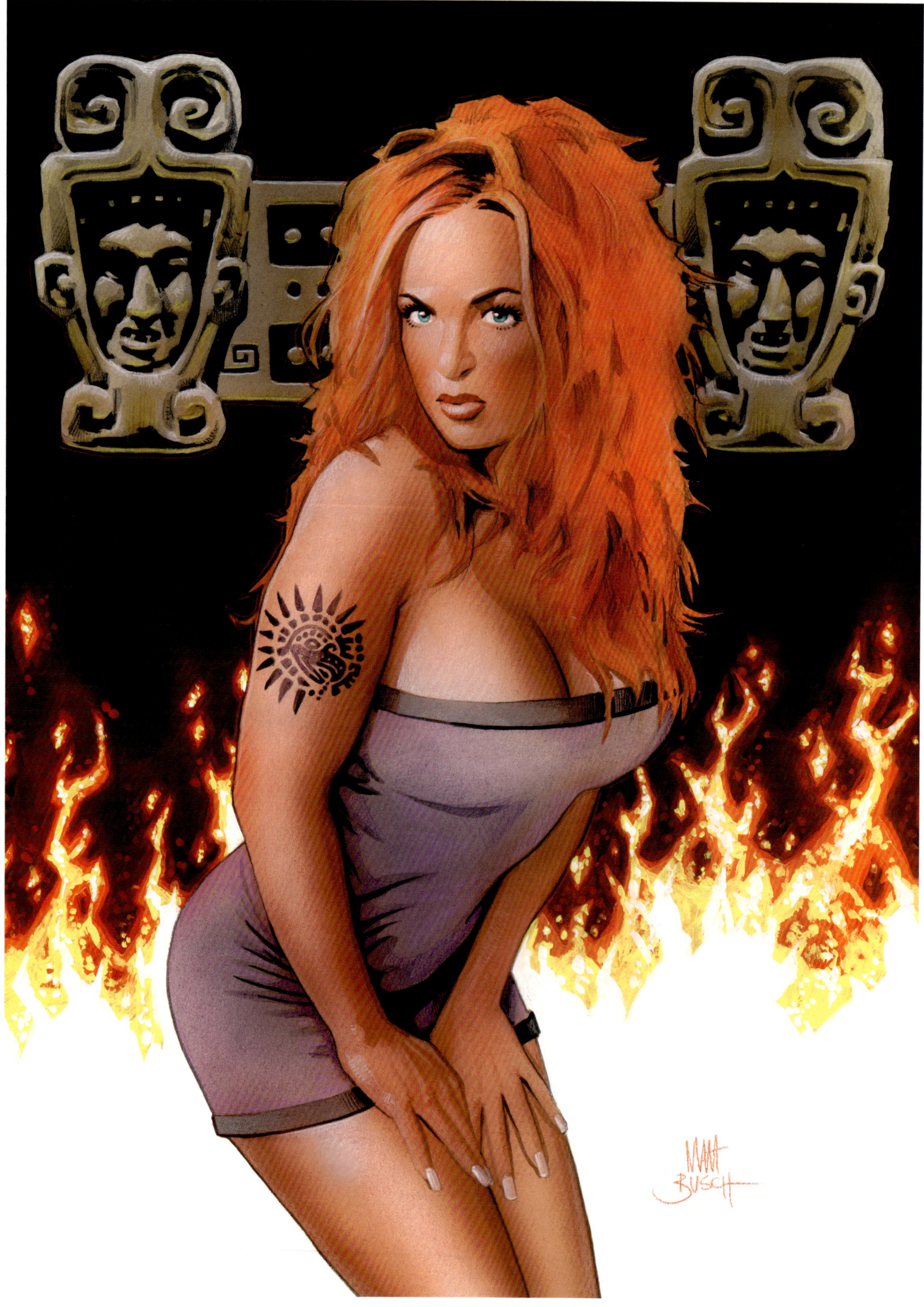
MATT
BUSCH

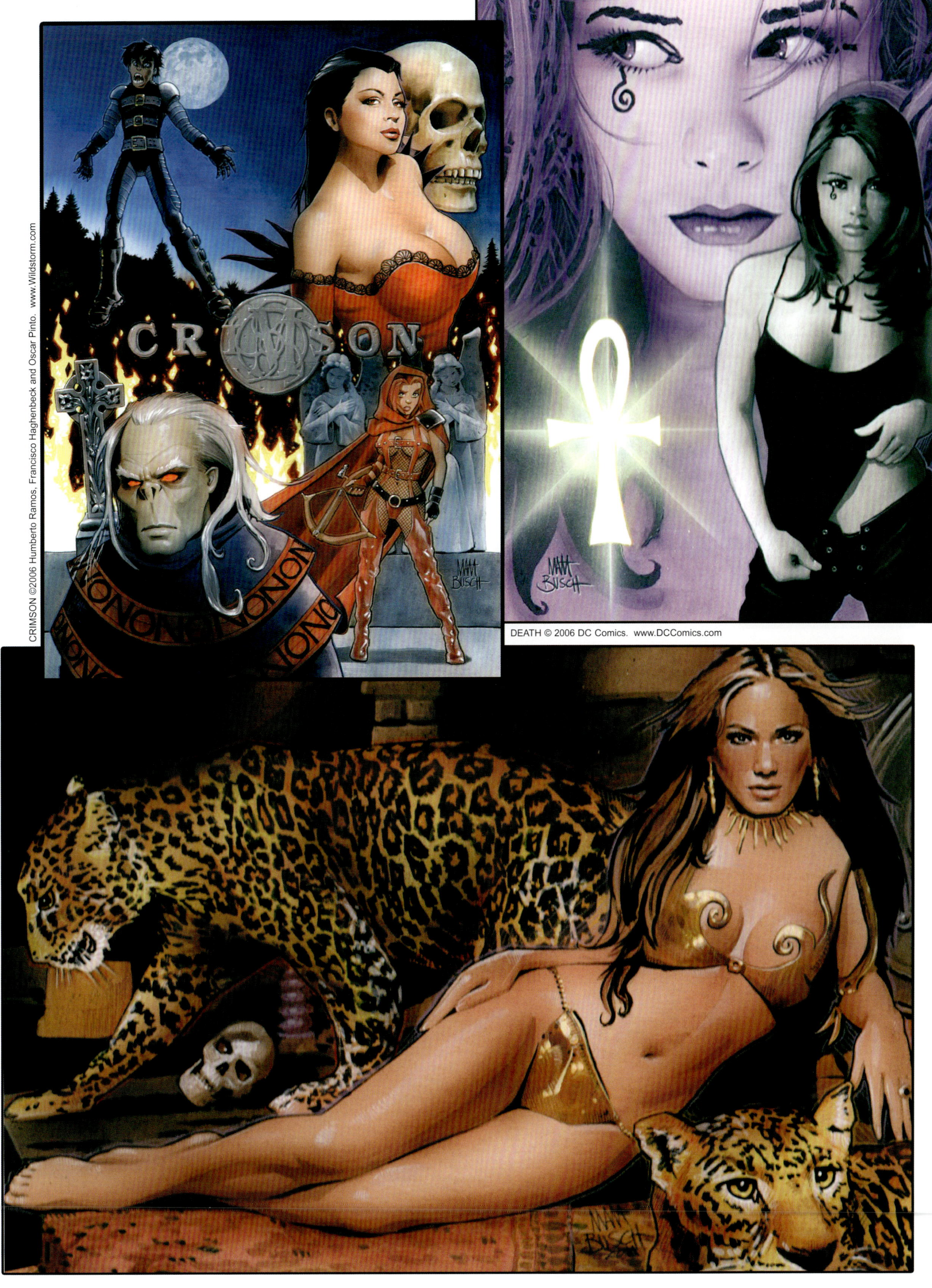

CRIMSON ©2006 Humberto Ramos, Francisco Haghenbeck and Oscar Pinto. www.Wildstorm.com

DEATH © 2006 DC Comics. www.DCComics.com

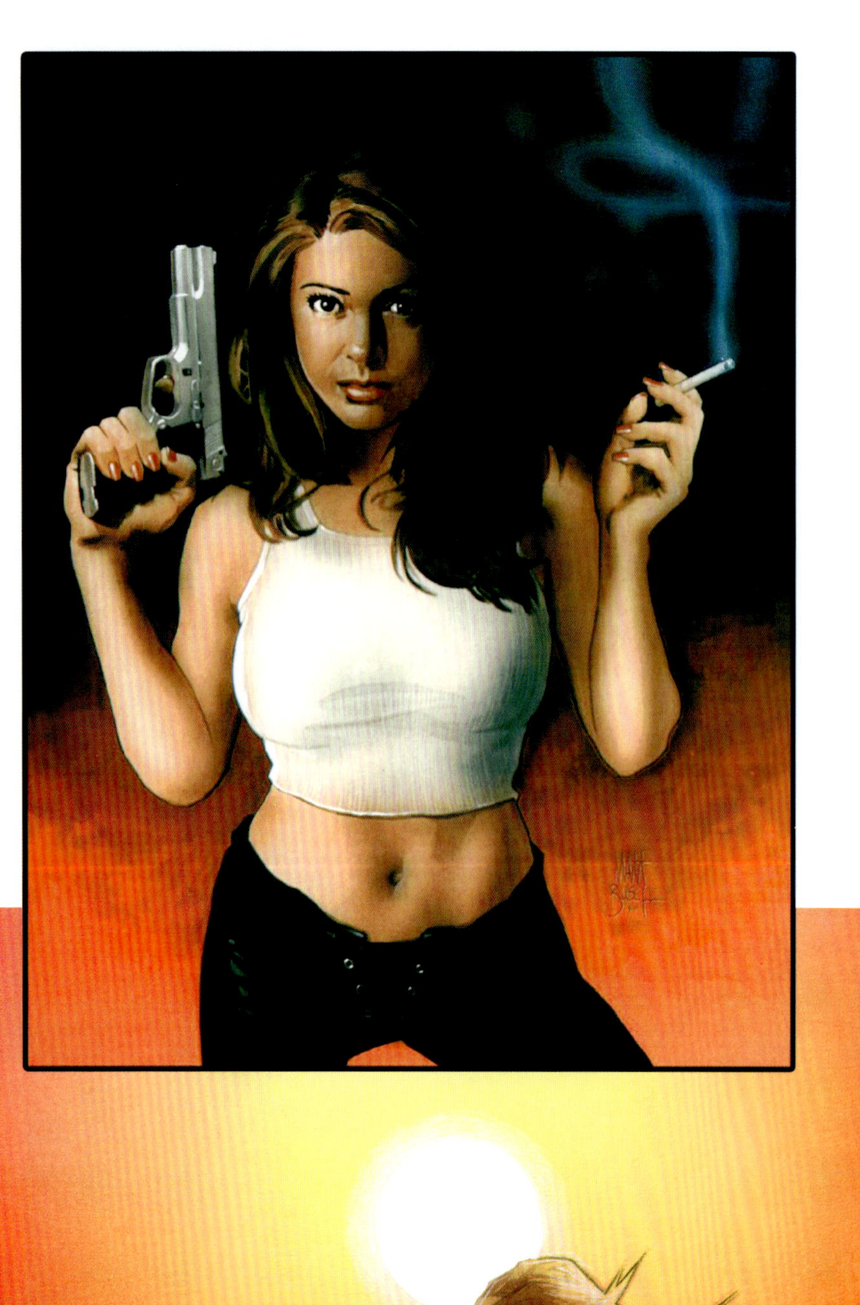

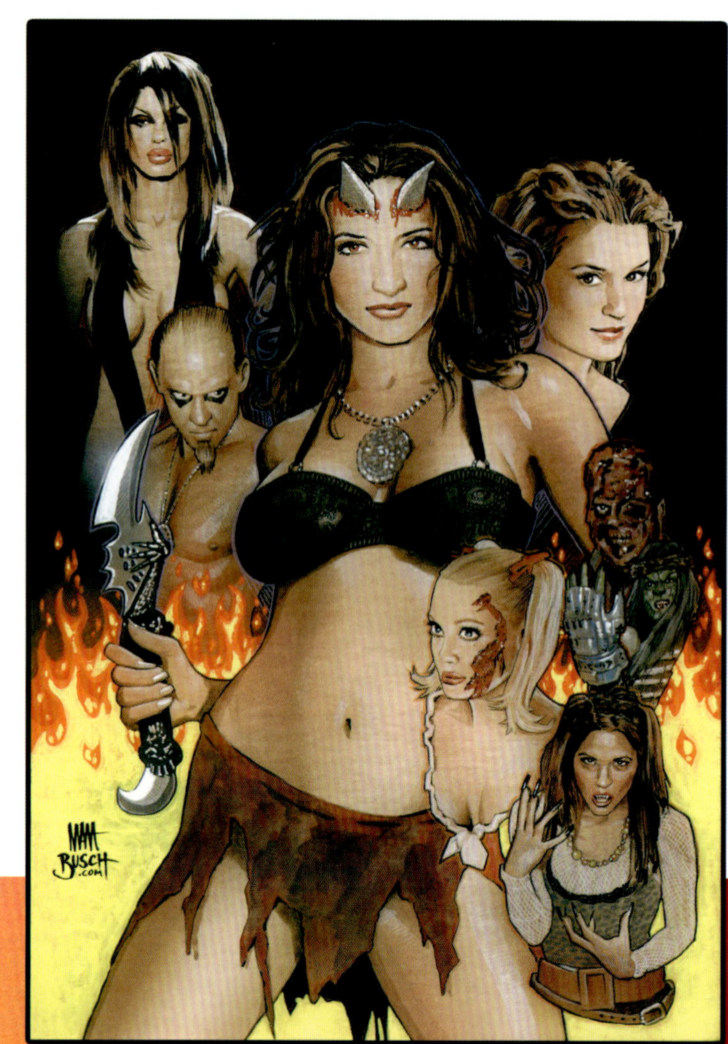

DEMONICA © 2006 Devil Girl Productions LP.

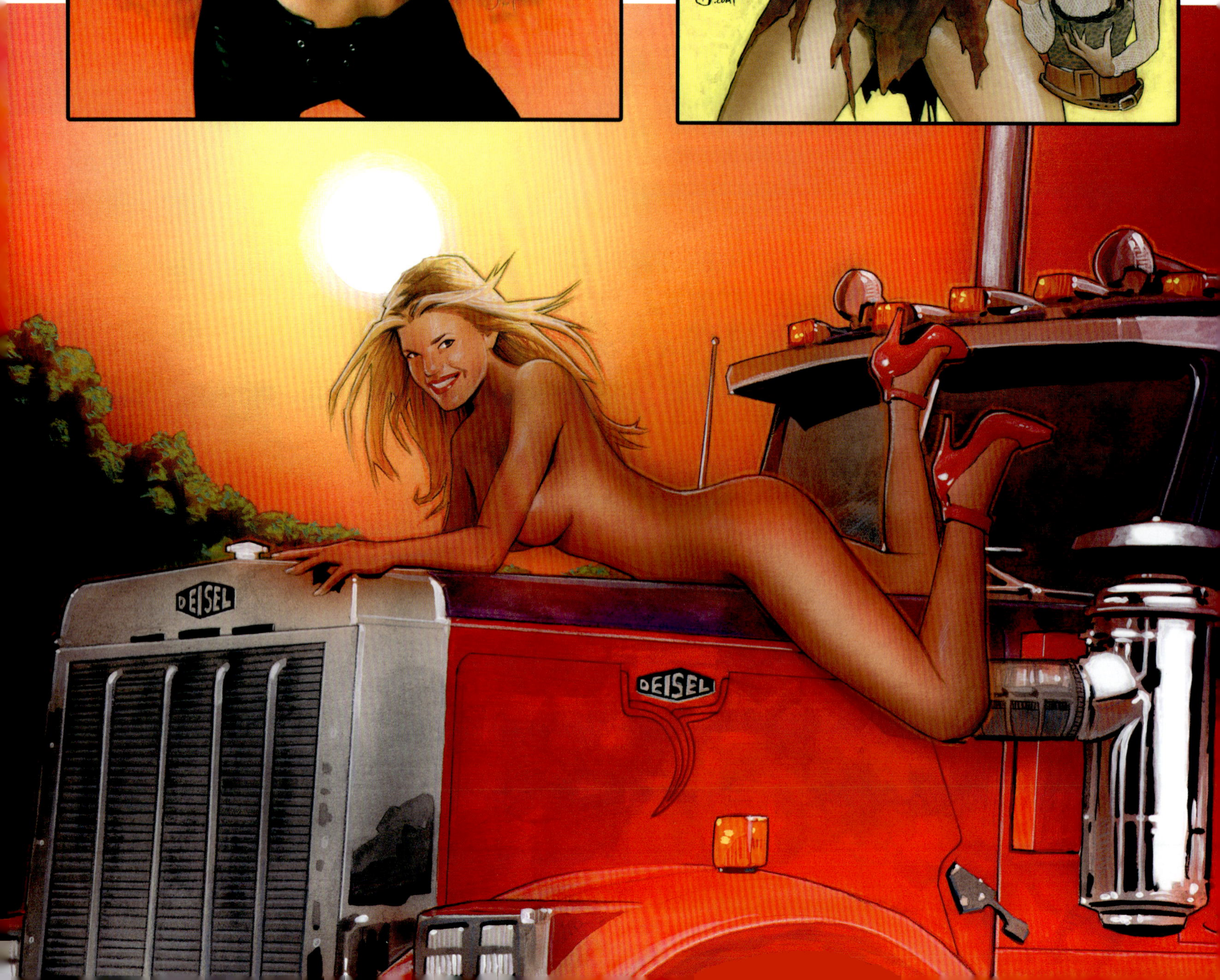

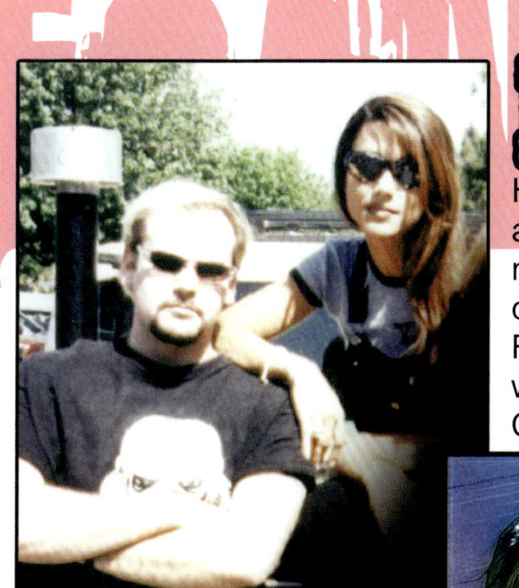

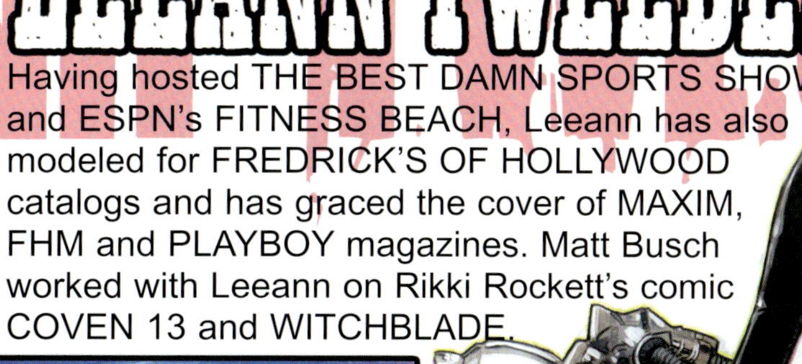

LEEANN TWEEDEN

Having hosted THE BEST DAMN SPORTS SHOW and ESPN's FITNESS BEACH, Leeann has also modeled for FREDRICK'S OF HOLLYWOOD catalogs and has graced the cover of MAXIM, FHM and PLAYBOY magazines. Matt Busch worked with Leeann on Rikki Rockett's comic COVEN 13 and WITCHBLADE.

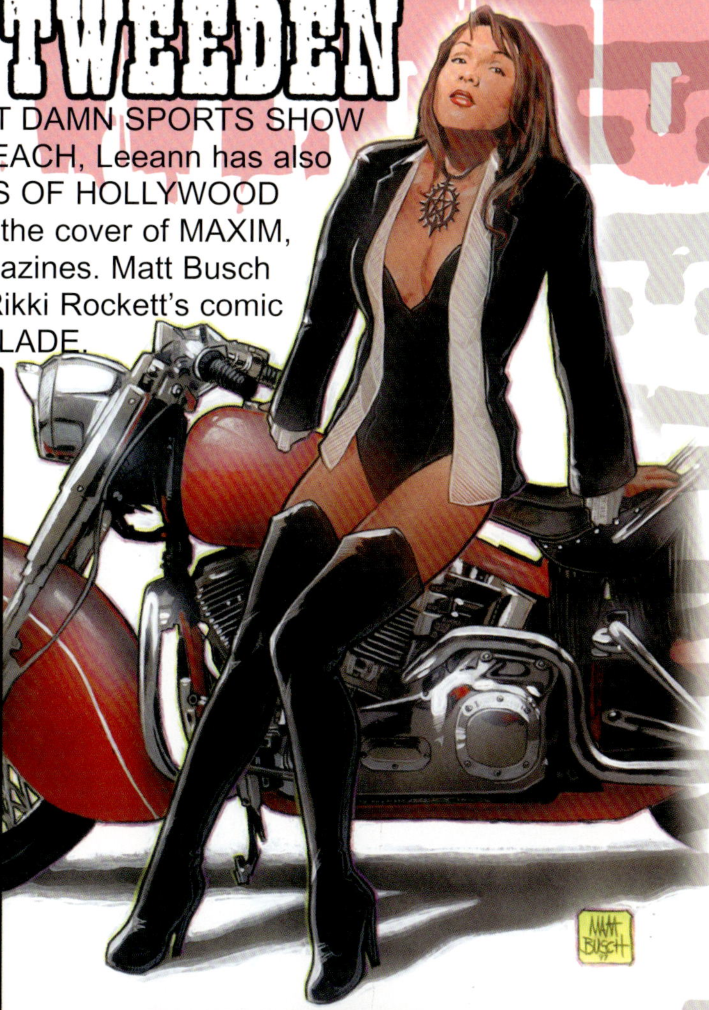

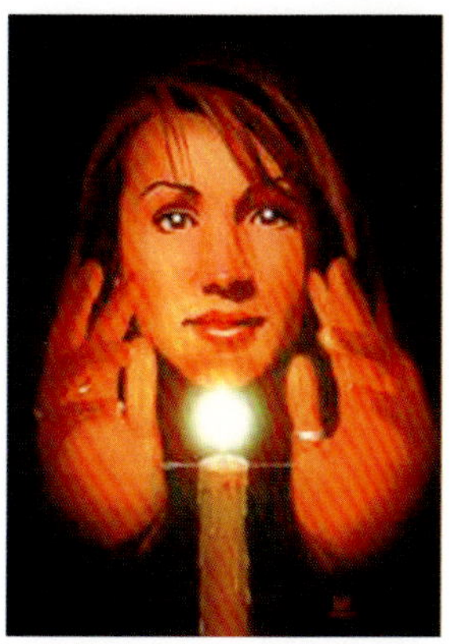

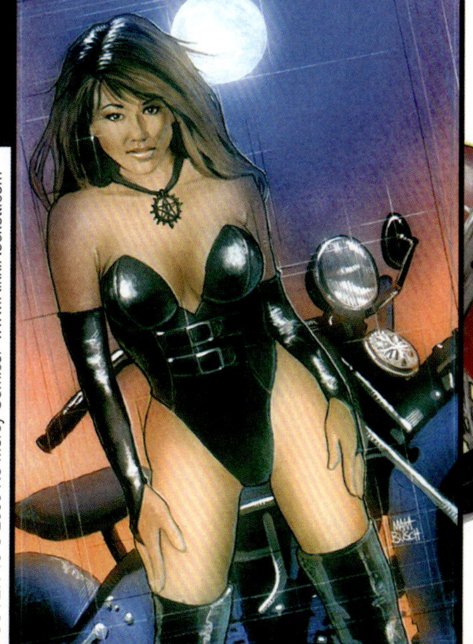

COVEN 13 © 2006 No Mercy Comics. www.RikkiRockett.com

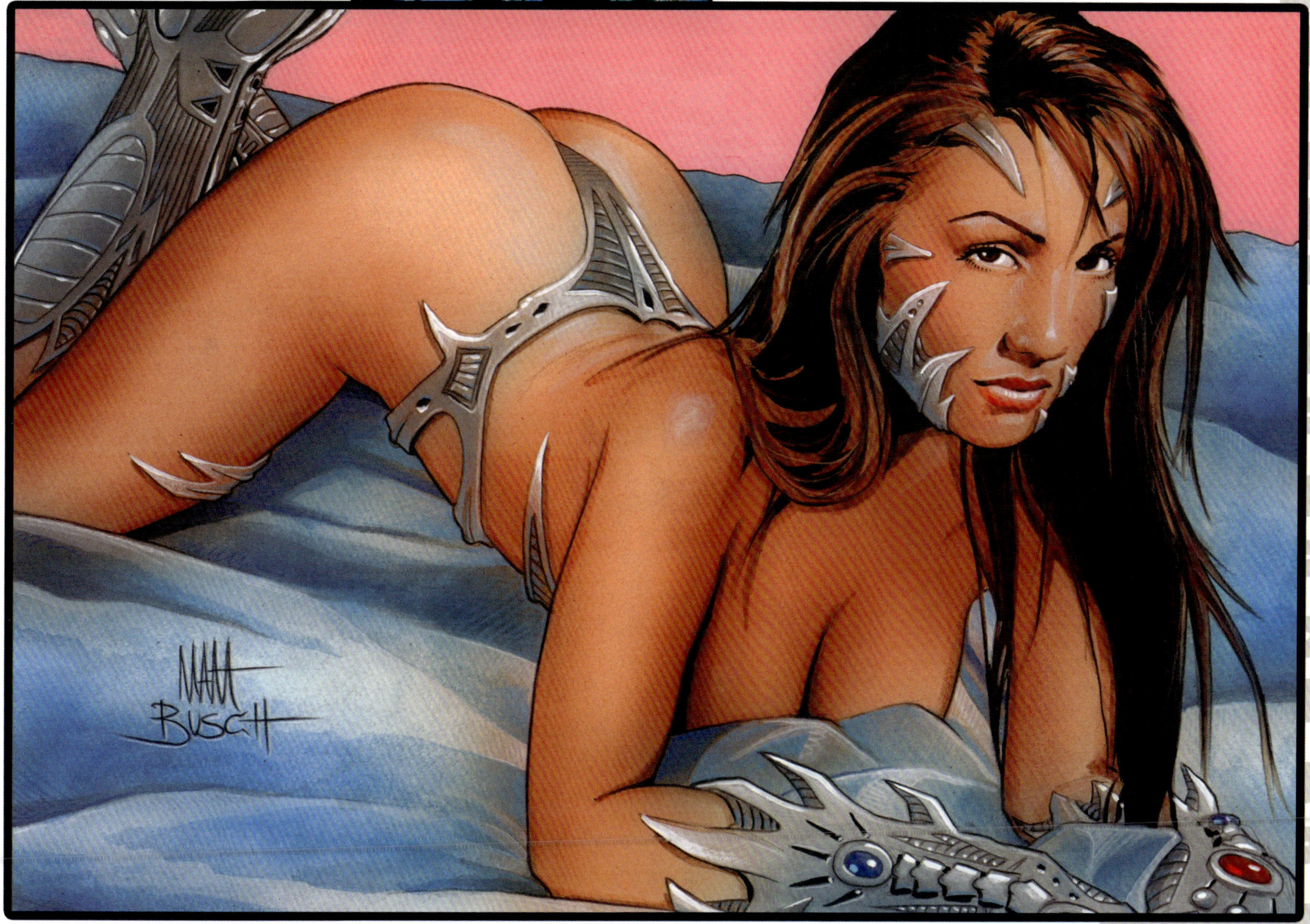

WITCHBLADE and APHRODITE IX © 2006 Top Cow Productions. www.TopCow.com

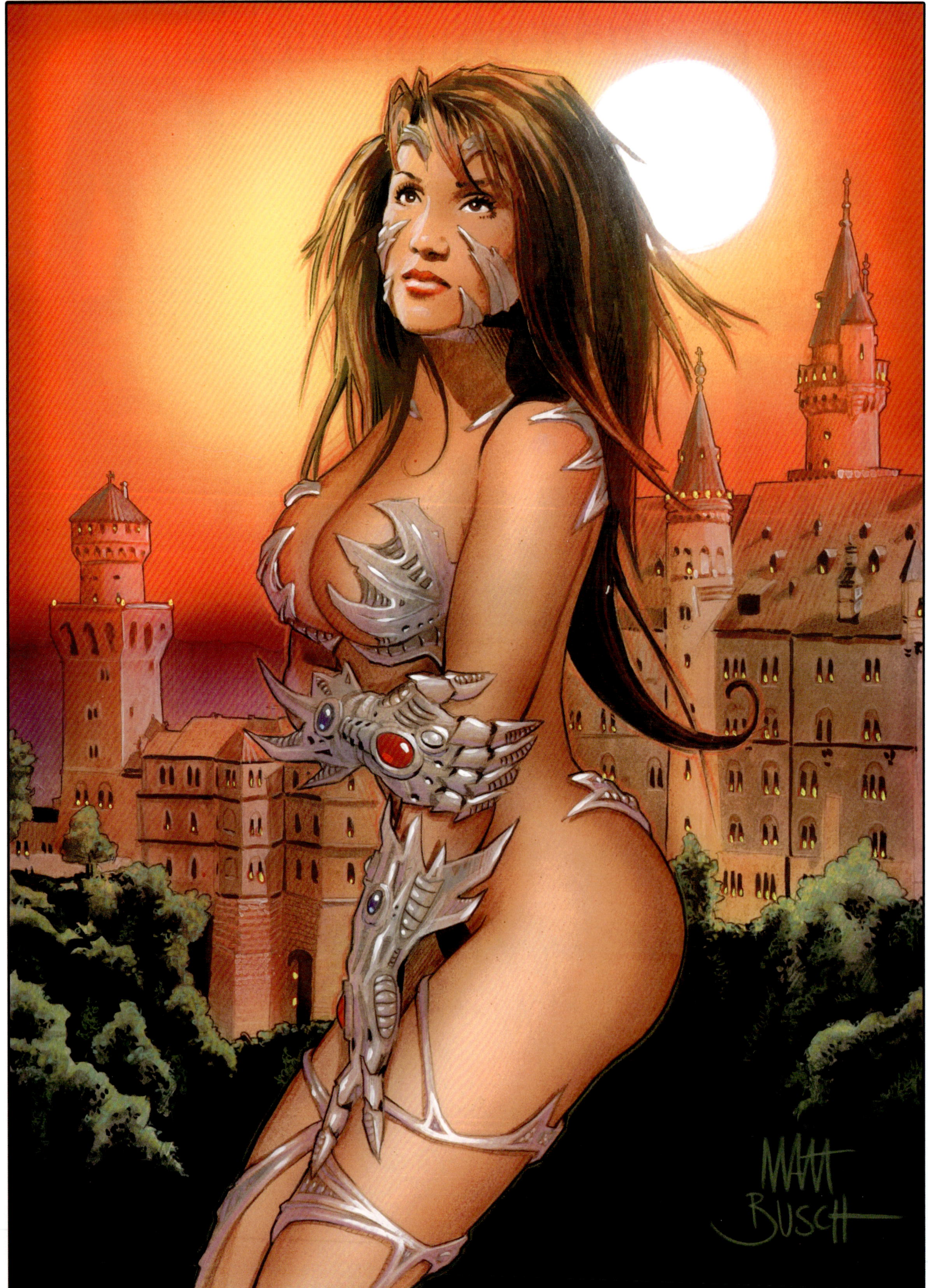
MATT BUSCH

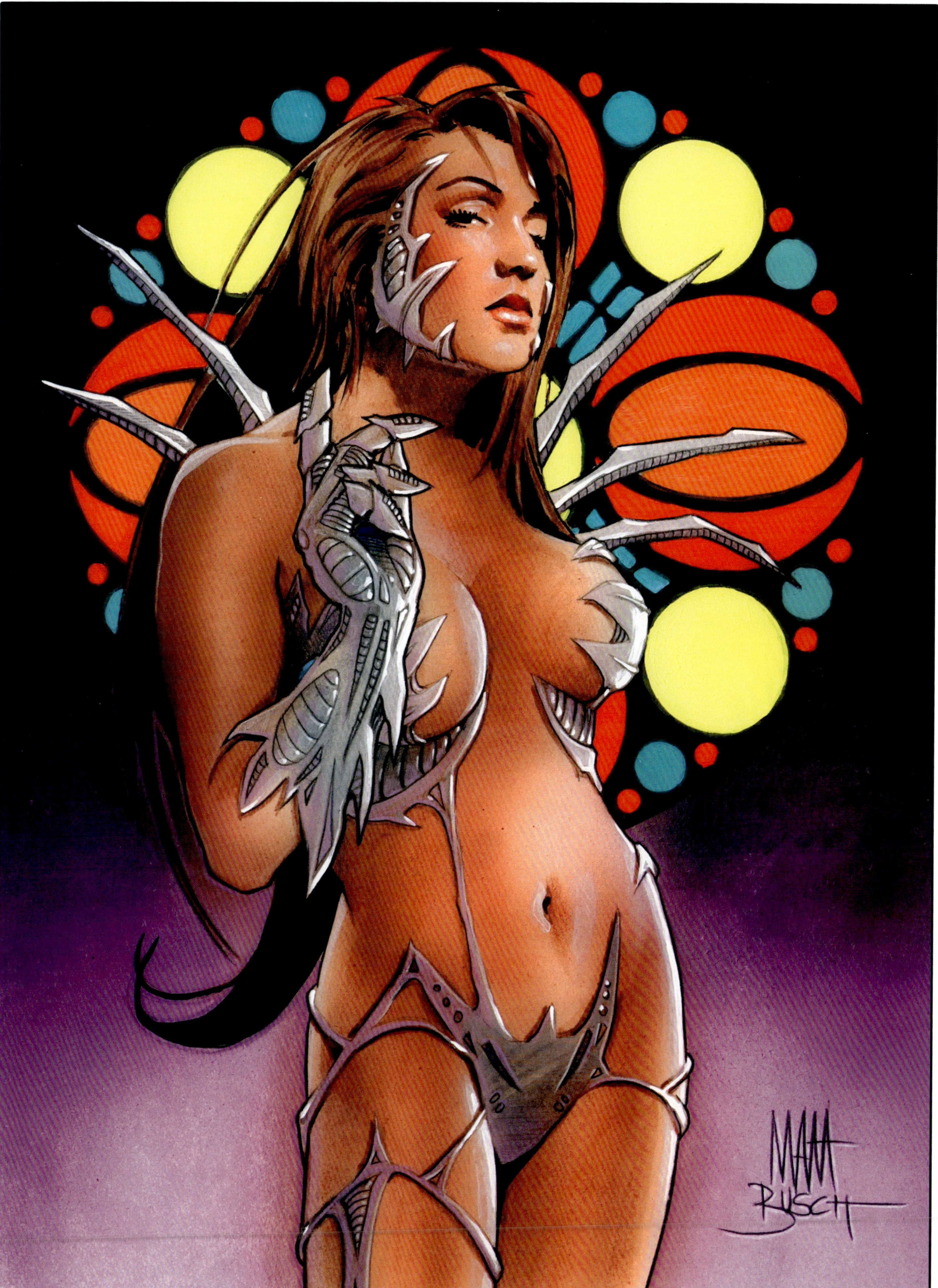

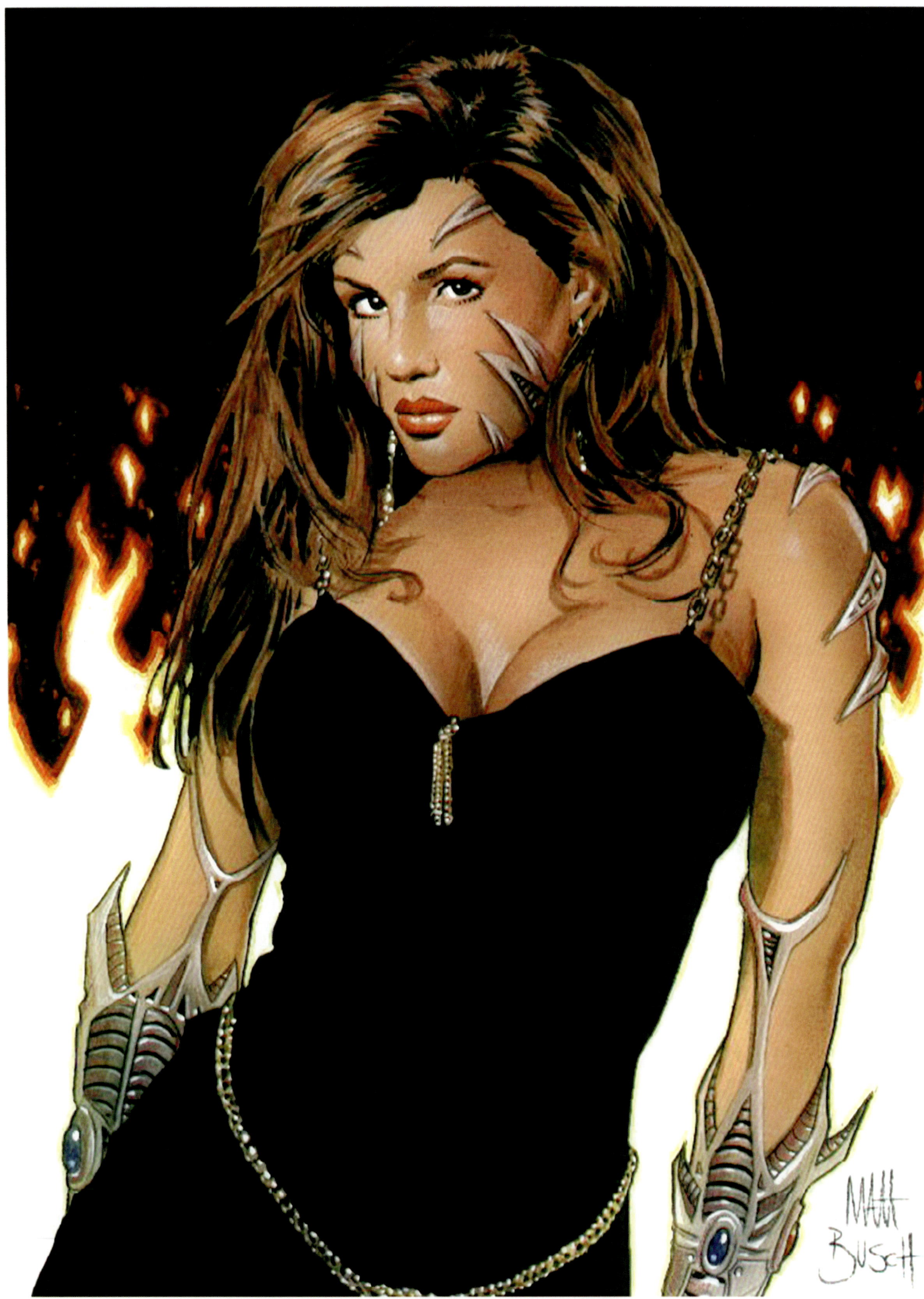
MATT
BUSCH

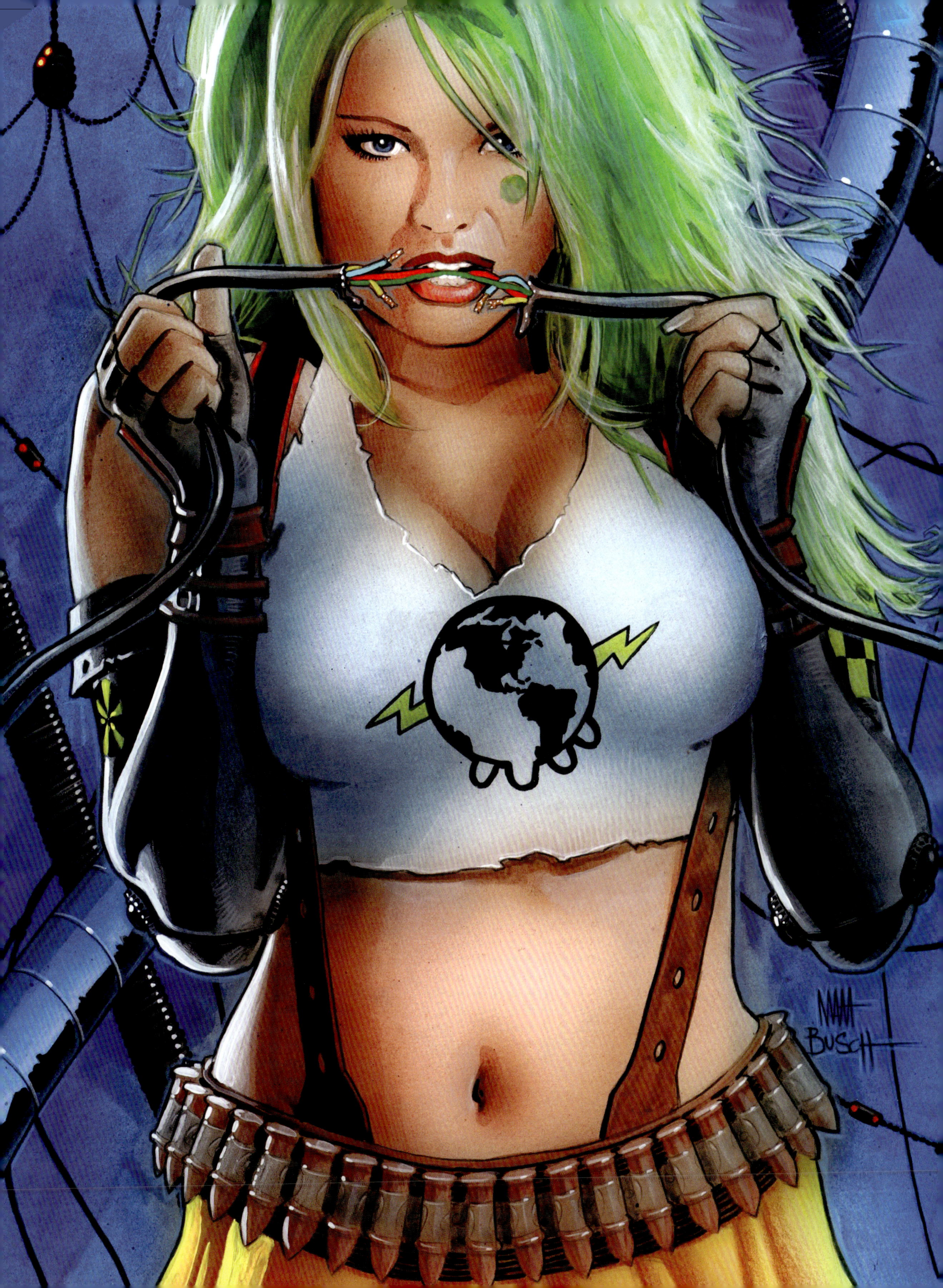
BUSCH

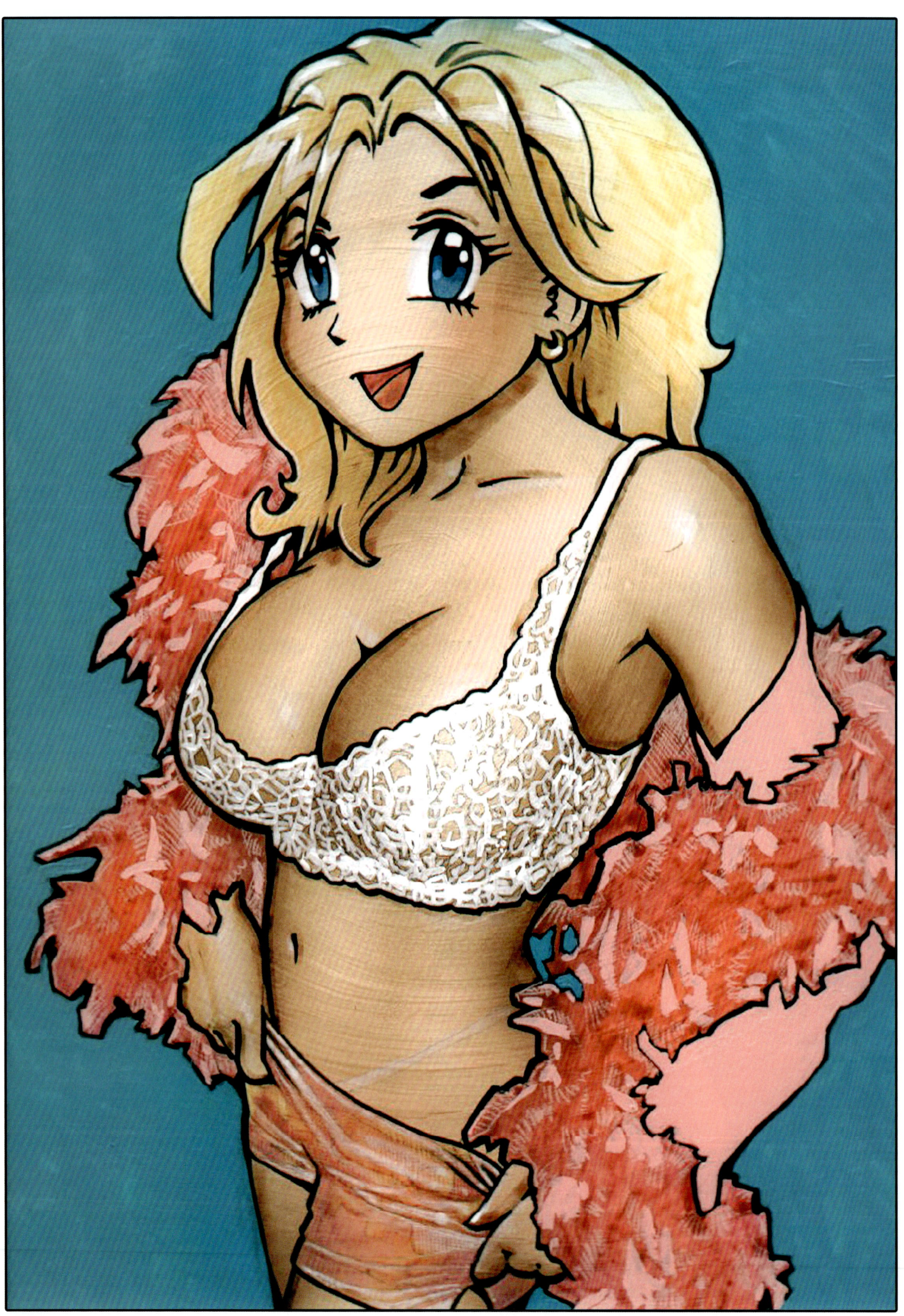

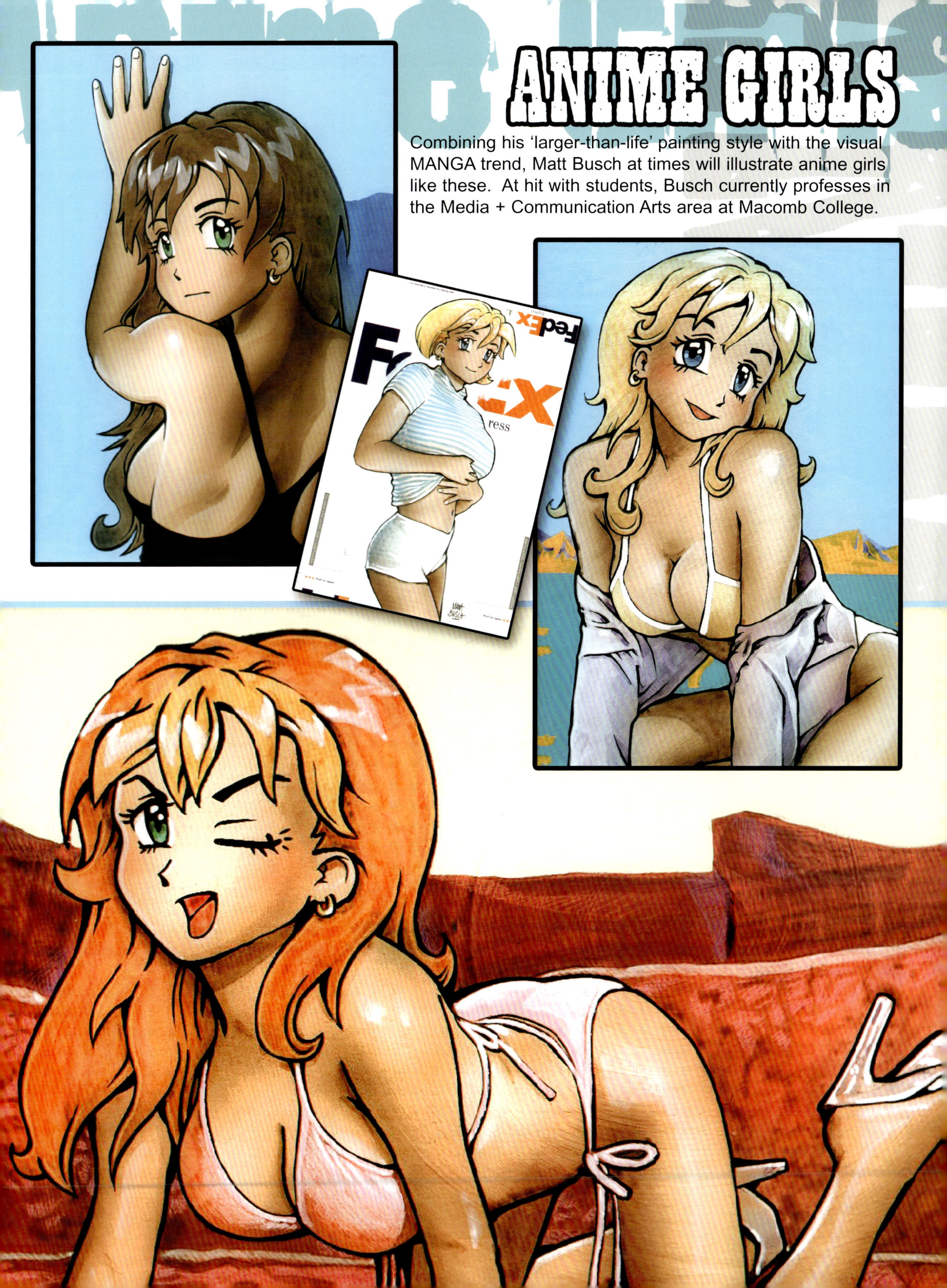

ANIME GIRLS

Combining his 'larger-than-life' painting style with the visual MANGA trend, Matt Busch at times will illustrate anime girls like these. At hit with students, Busch currently professes in the Media + Communication Arts area at Macomb College.

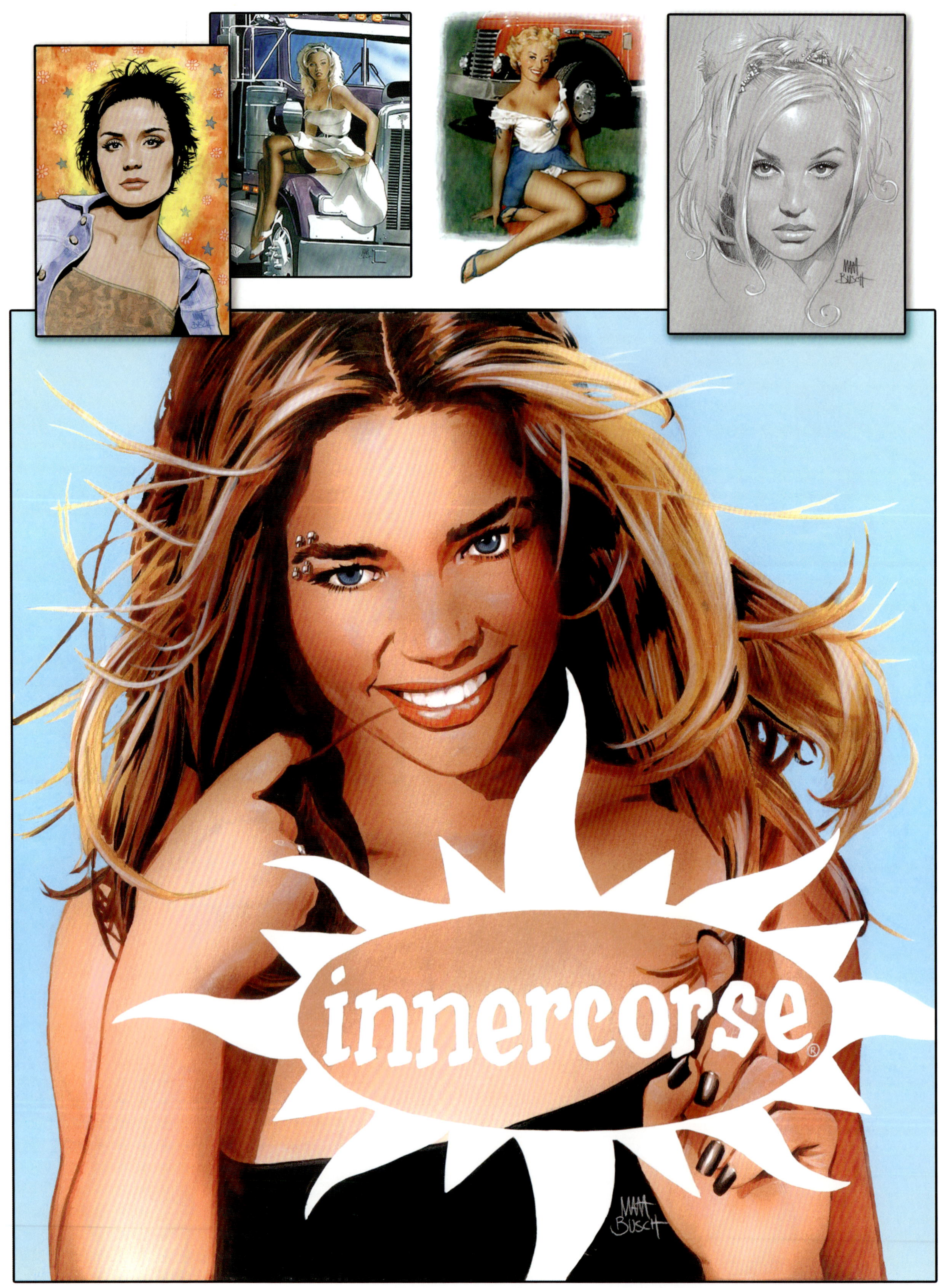
innercorse®
MATT BUSCH

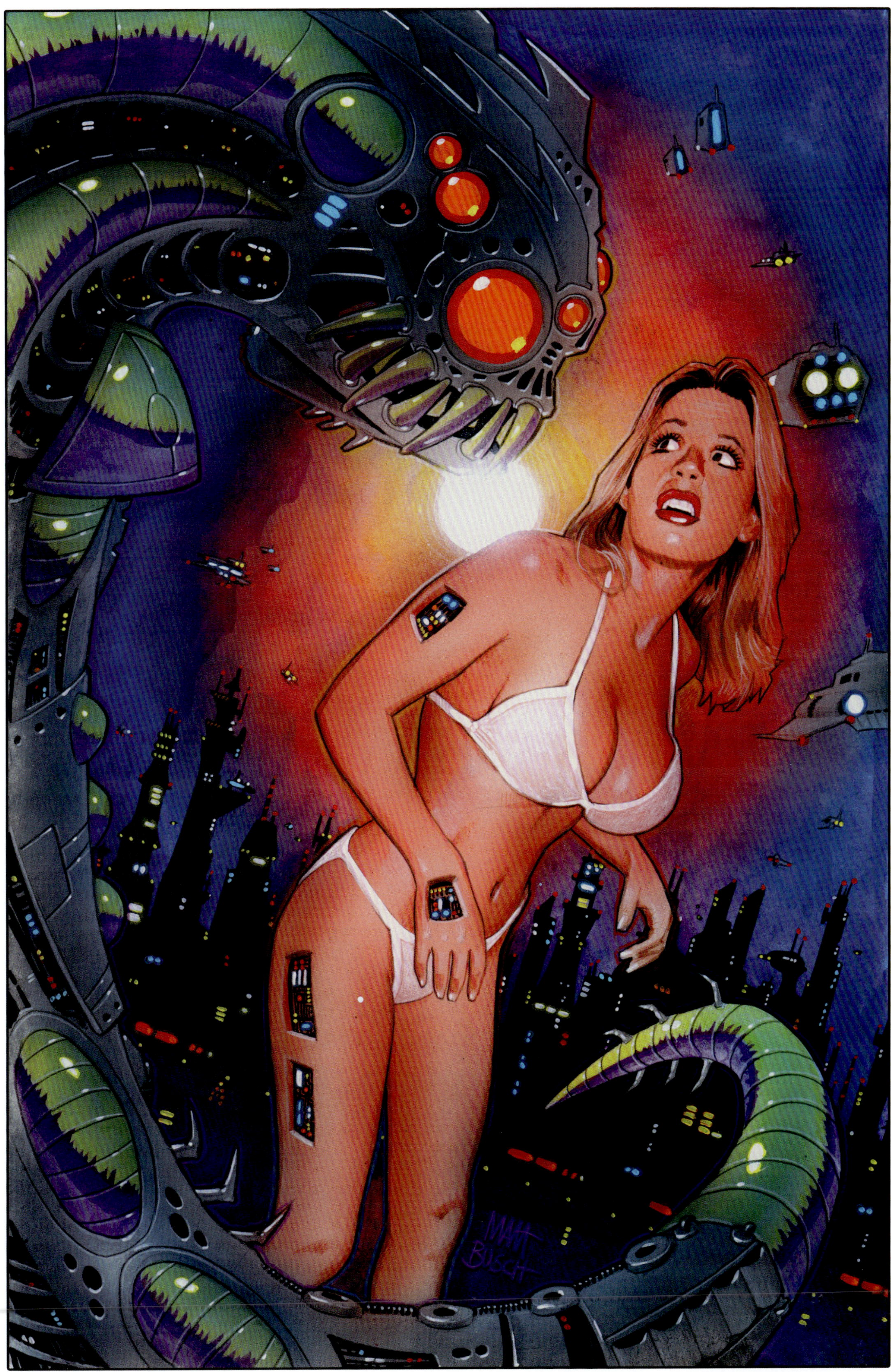

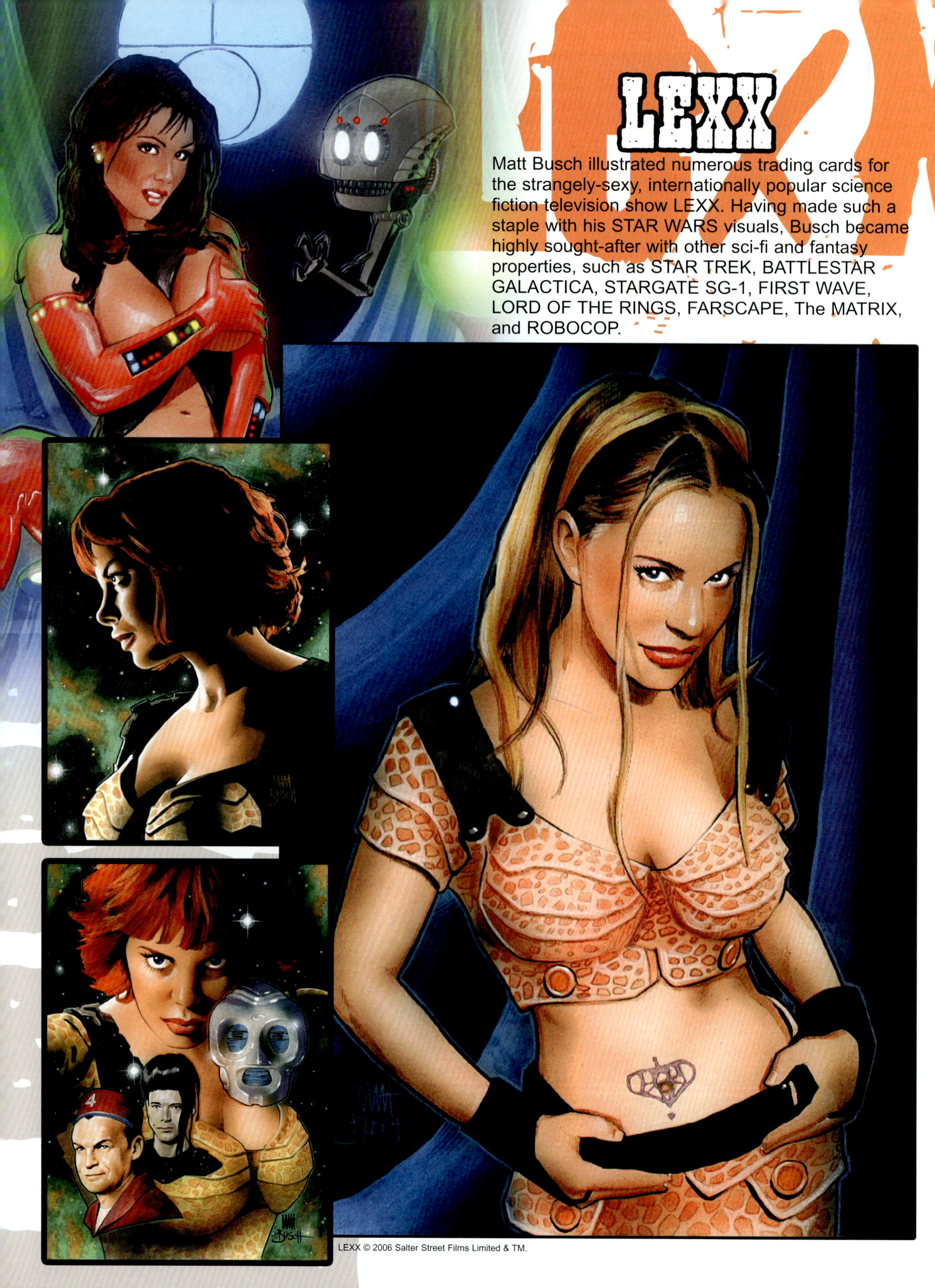

LEXX

Matt Busch illustrated numerous trading cards for the strangely-sexy, internationally popular science fiction television show LEXX. Having made such a staple with his STAR WARS visuals, Busch became highly sought-after with other sci-fi and fantasy properties, such as STAR TREK, BATTLESTAR GALACTICA, STARGATE SG-1, FIRST WAVE, LORD OF THE RINGS, FARSCAPE, The MATRIX, and ROBOCOP.

LEXX © 2006 Salter Street Films Limited & TM.

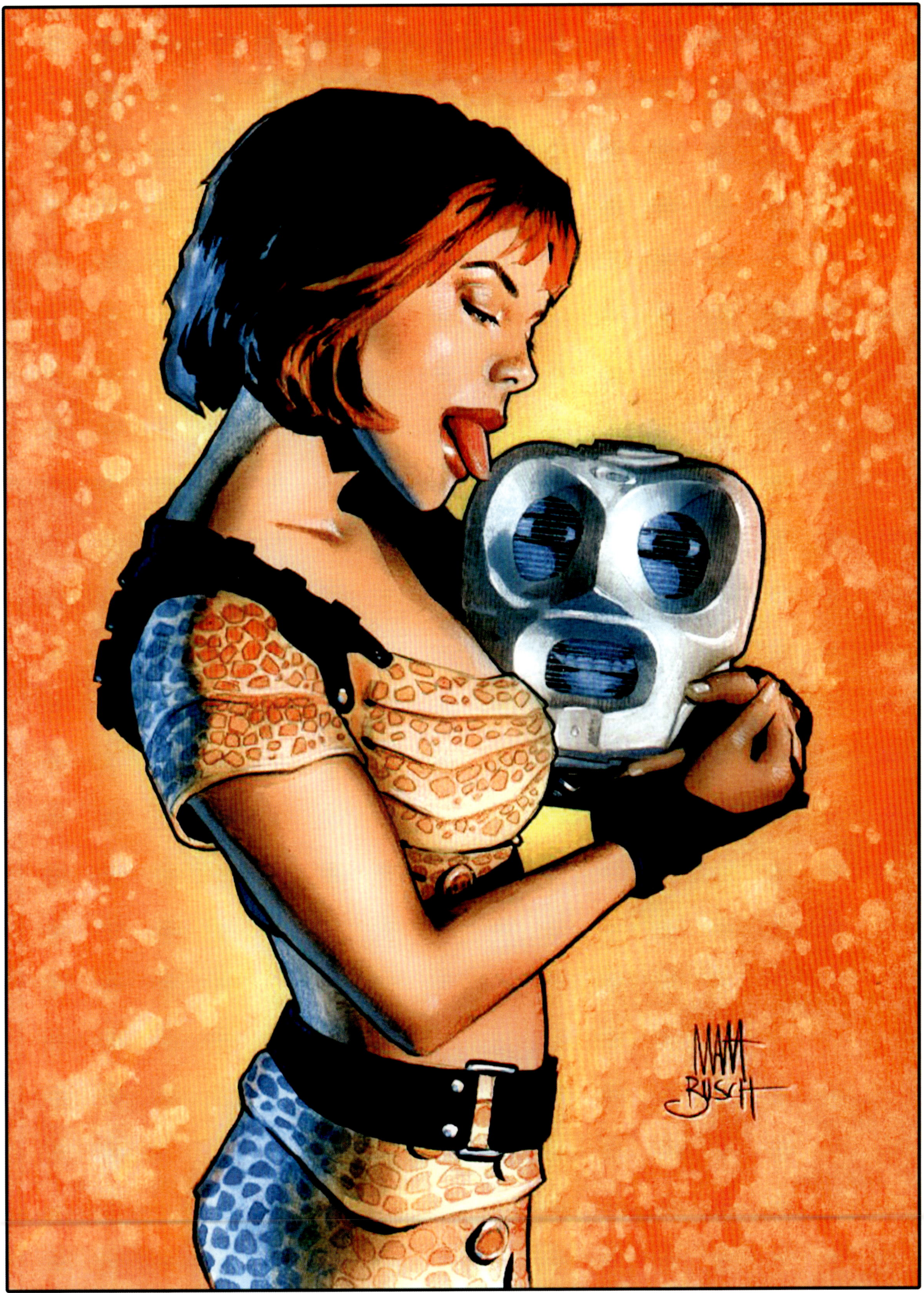

LISA MARIE SCOTT

Another popular model that Matt Busch has worked with several times is Lisa Marie Scott. Mostly known for her PLAYBOY pictorials, Lisa has also posed for such magazines as FHM and VANITY FAIR. Lisa has also dabbled in acting, having played parts in such television shows as BAYWATCH NIGHTS and MARRIED... WITH CHILDREN.

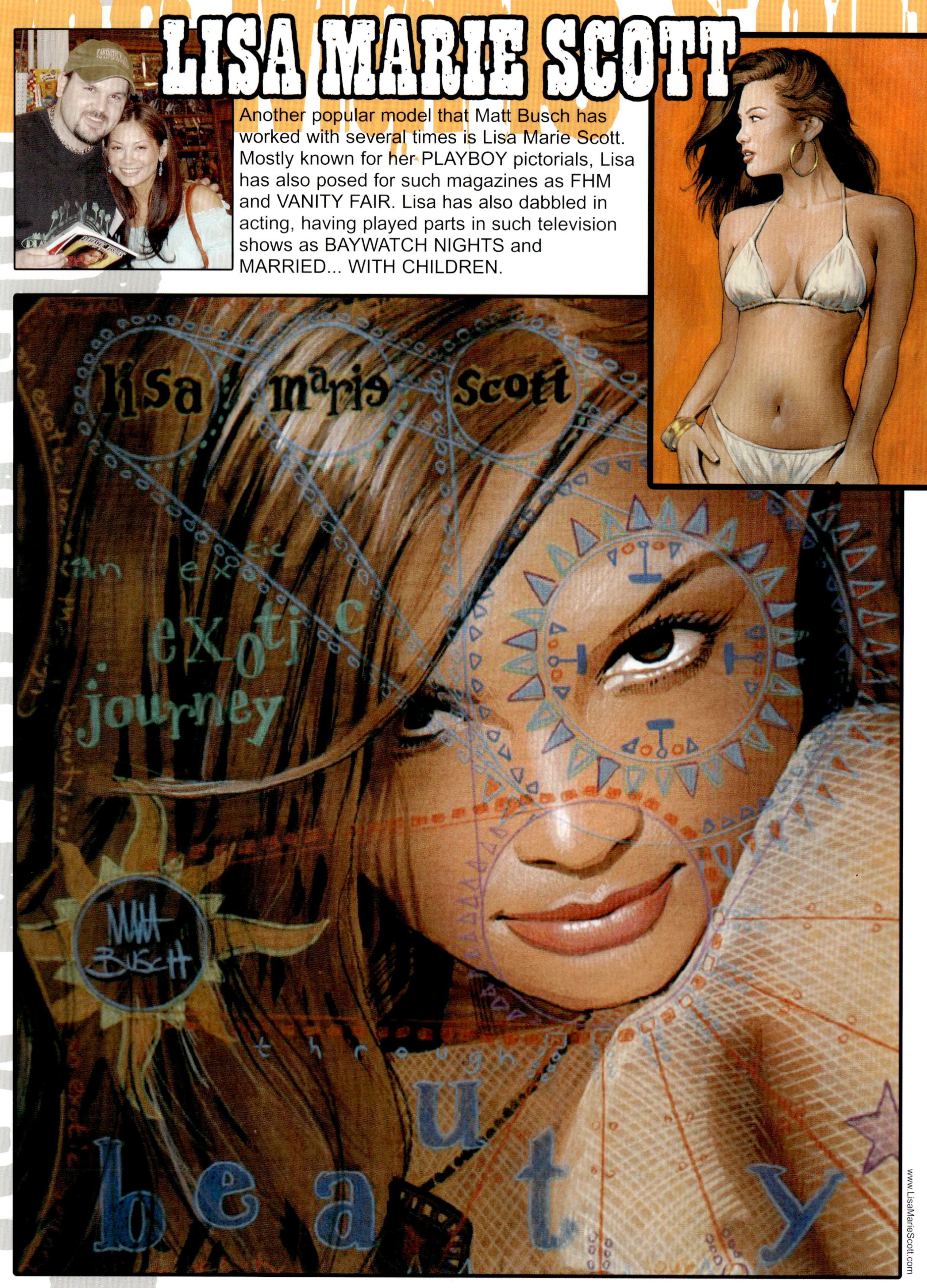

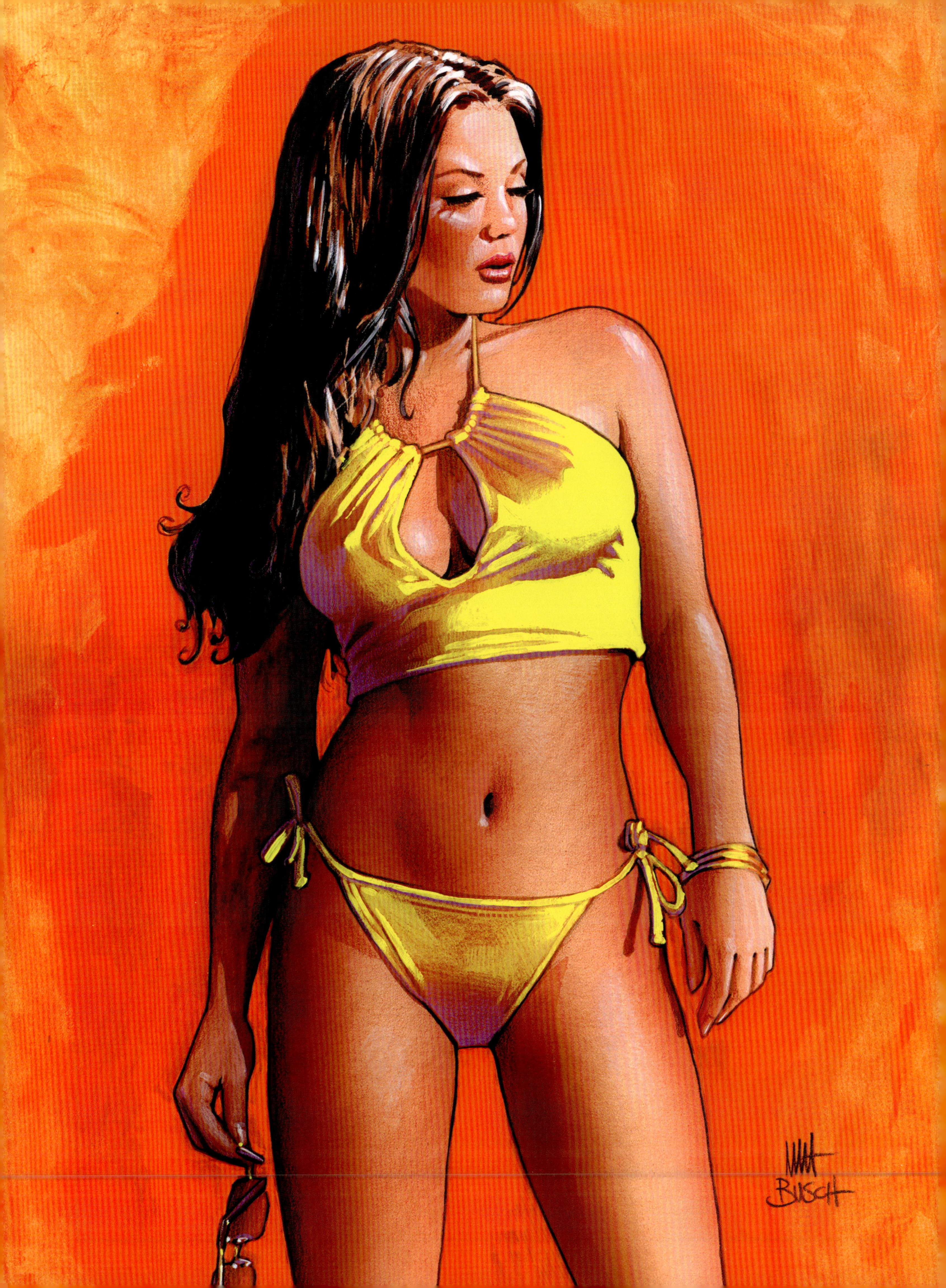
BUSCH

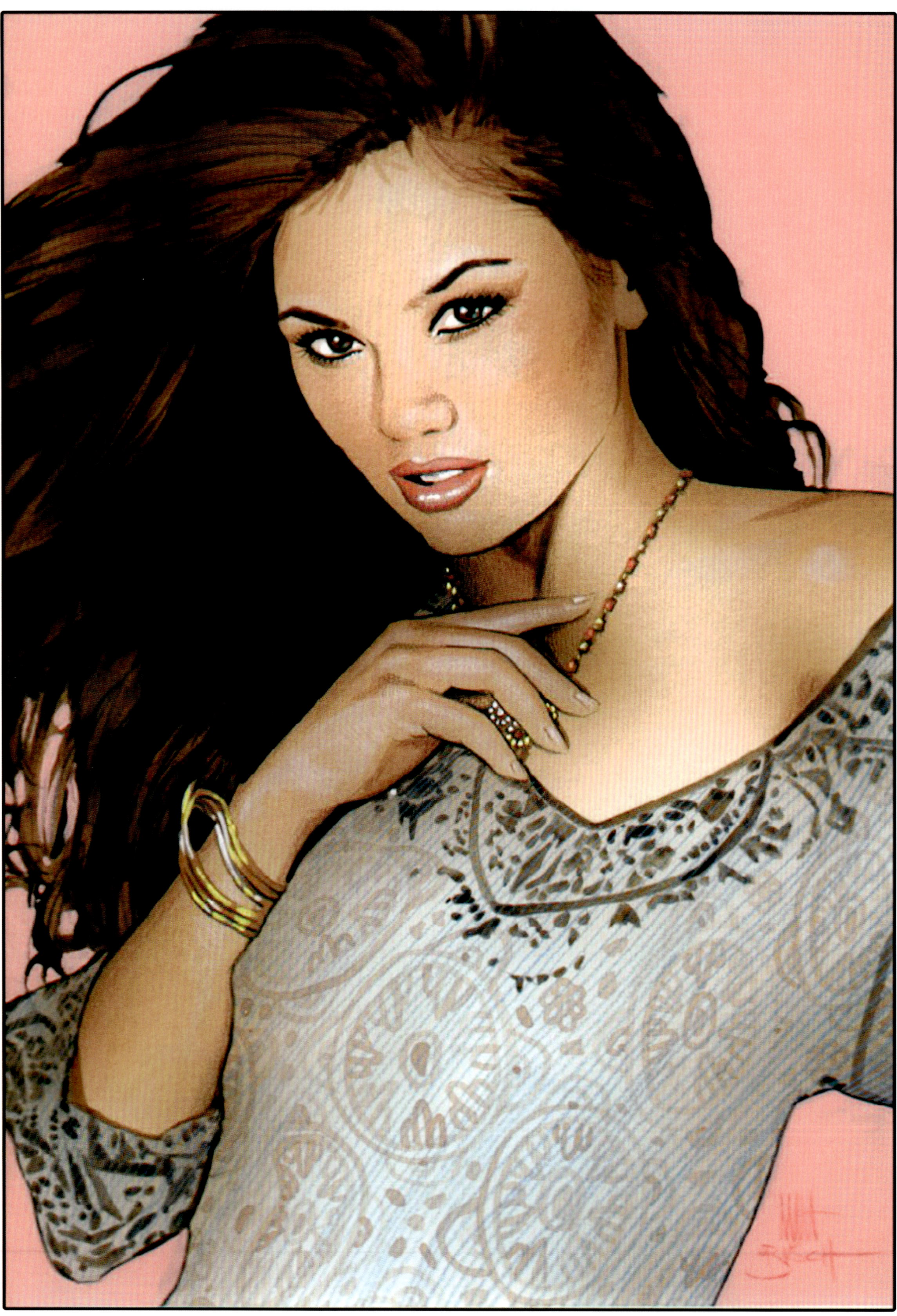

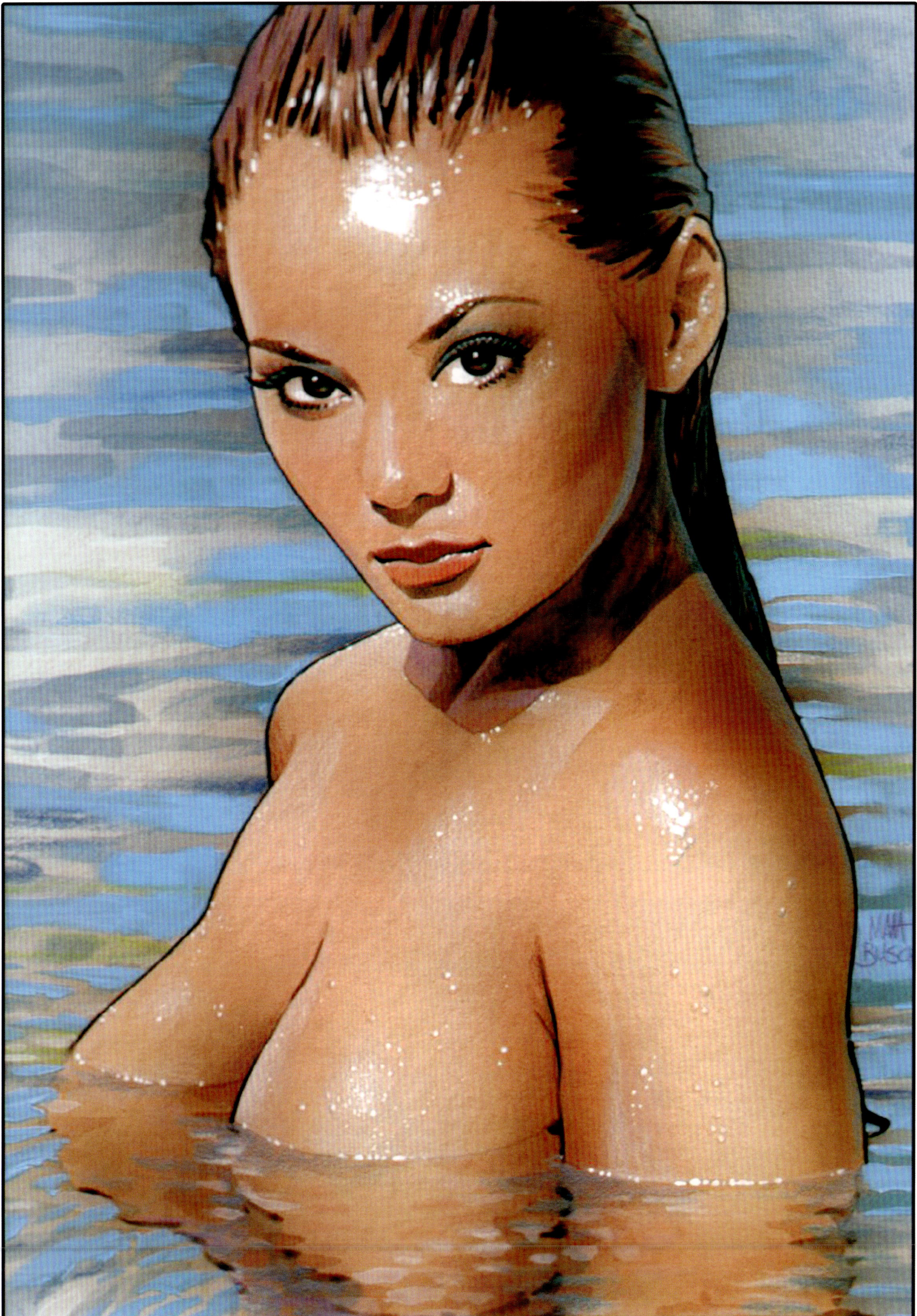

LADY DEATH

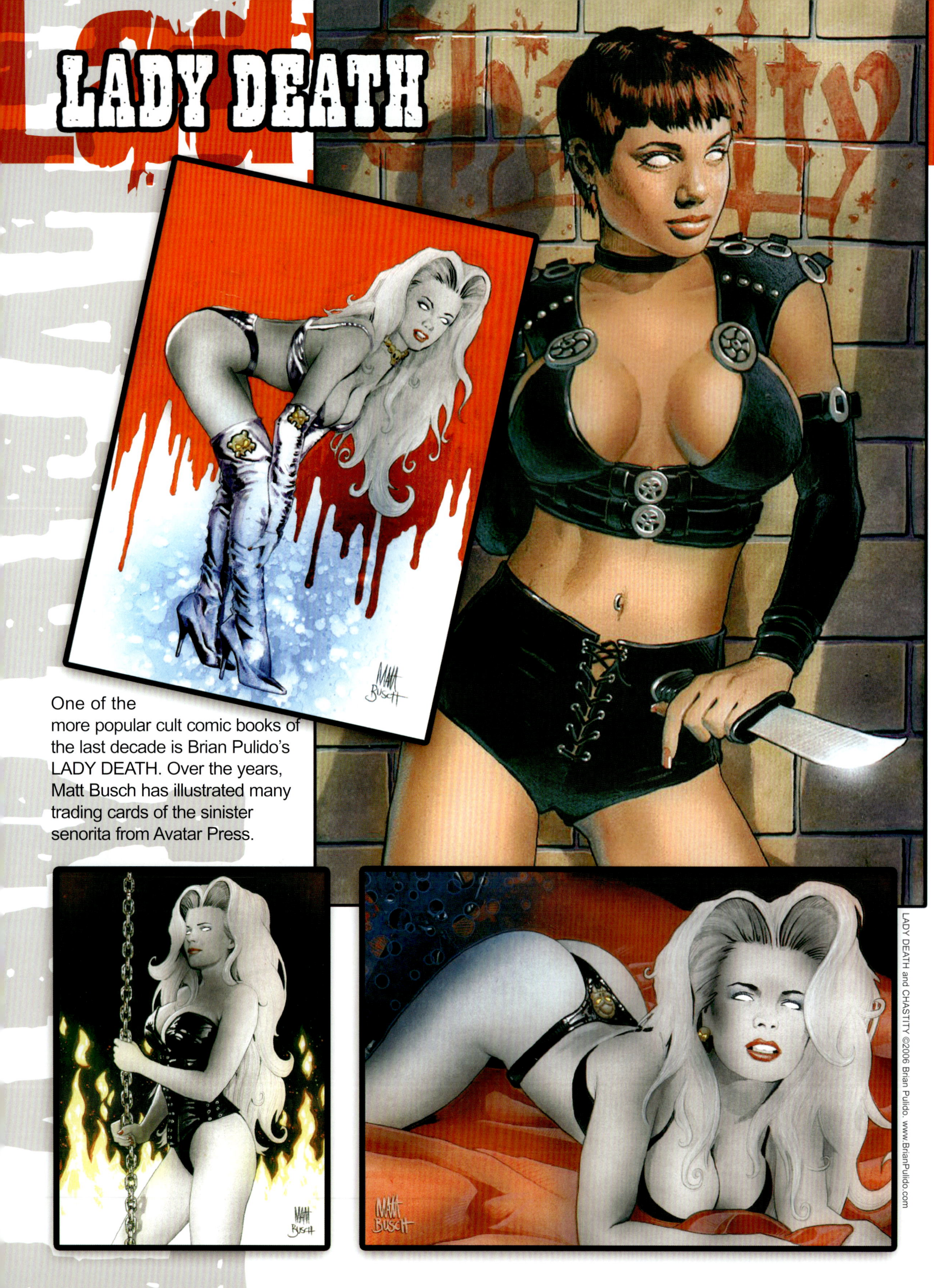

One of the more popular cult comic books of the last decade is Brian Pulido's LADY DEATH. Over the years, Matt Busch has illustrated many trading cards of the sinister senorita from Avatar Press.

LADY DEATH and CHASTITY ©2006 Brian Pulido. www.BrianPulido.com

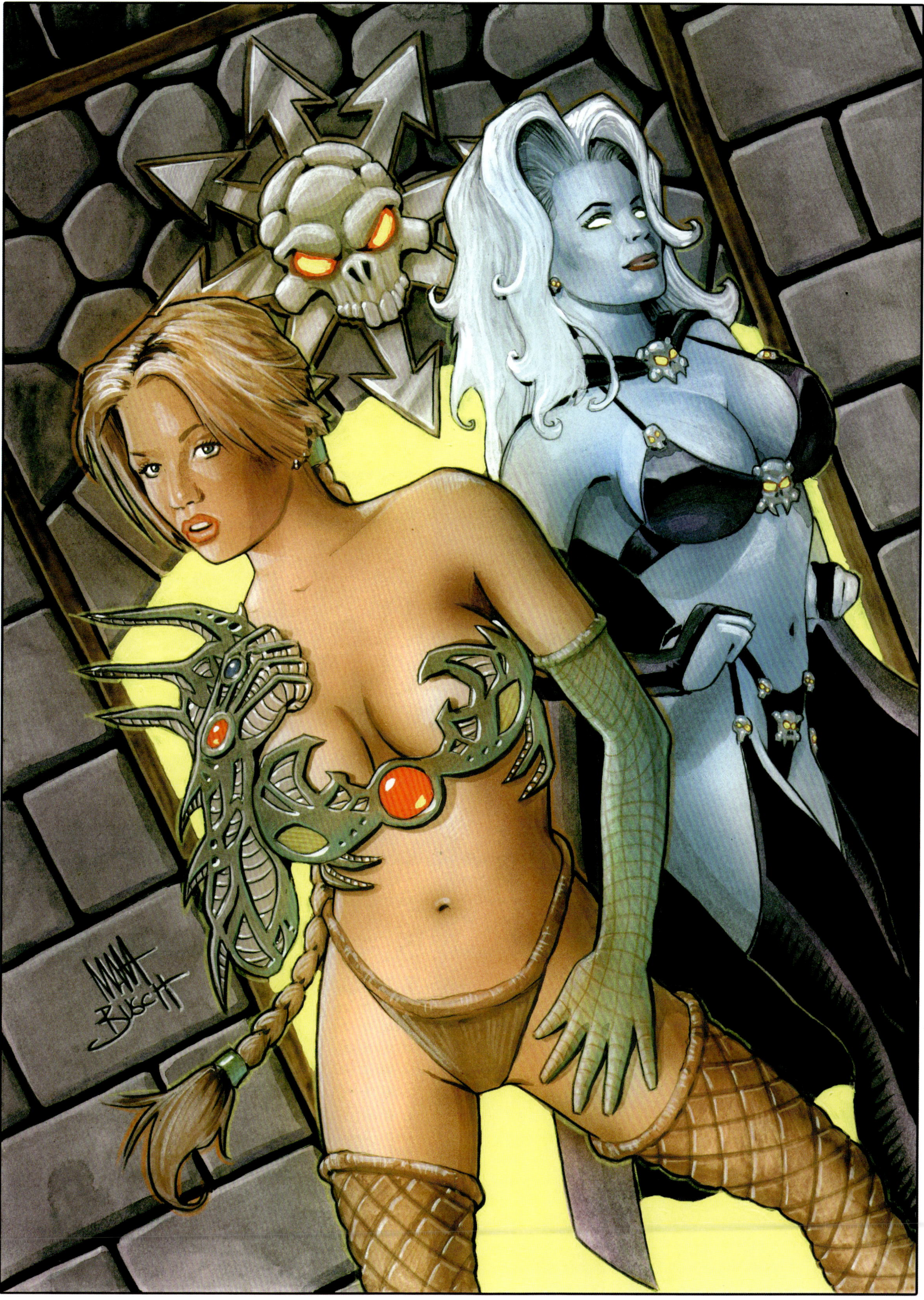

CREATING A FANTASY

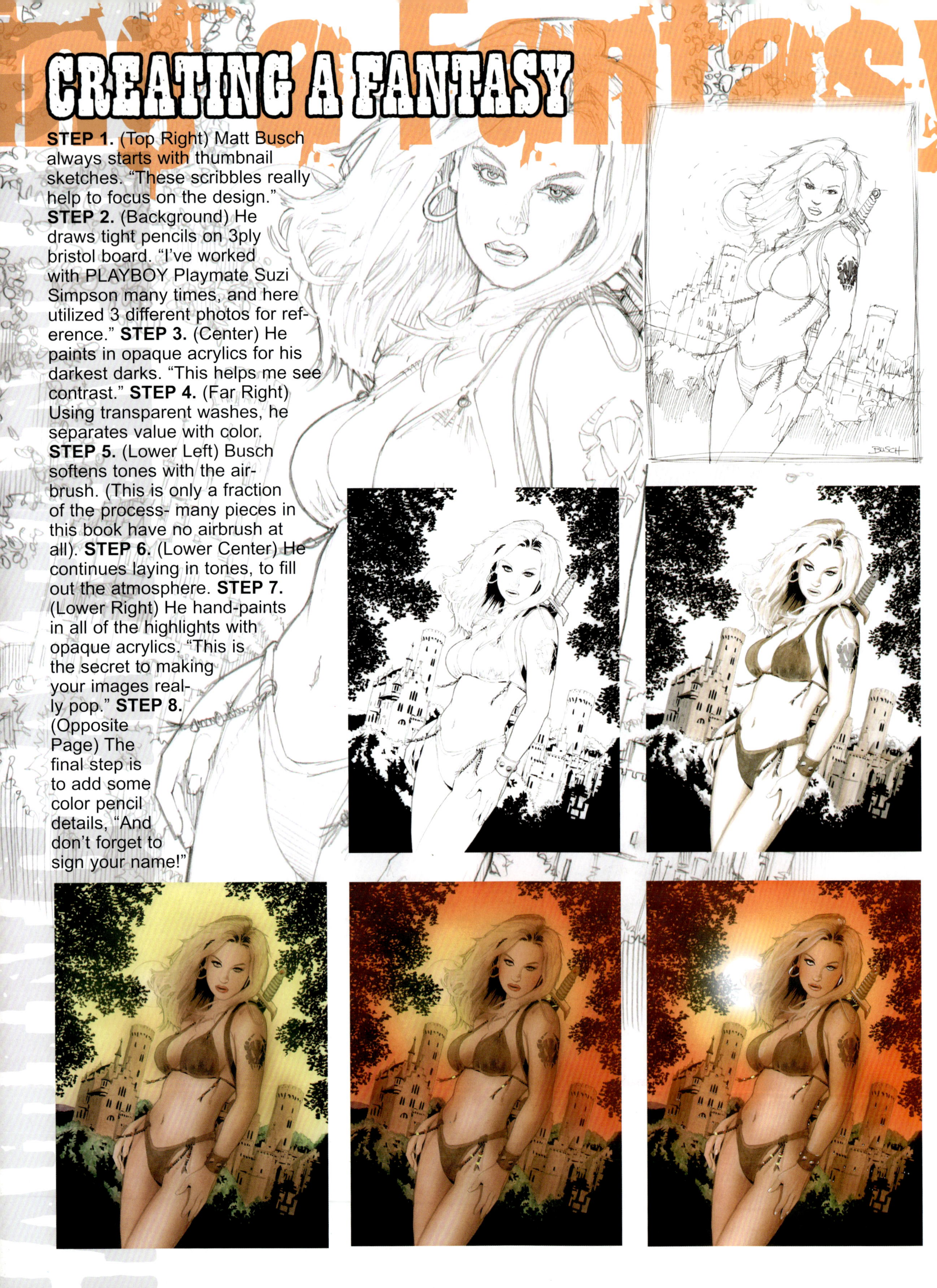

STEP 1. (Top Right) Matt Busch always starts with thumbnail sketches. "These scribbles really help to focus on the design." **STEP 2.** (Background) He draws tight pencils on 3ply bristol board. "I've worked with PLAYBOY Playmate Suzi Simpson many times, and here utilized 3 different photos for reference." **STEP 3.** (Center) He paints in opaque acrylics for his darkest darks. "This helps me see contrast." **STEP 4.** (Far Right) Using transparent washes, he separates value with color. **STEP 5.** (Lower Left) Busch softens tones with the airbrush. (This is only a fraction of the process- many pieces in this book have no airbrush at all). **STEP 6.** (Lower Center) He continues laying in tones, to fill out the atmosphere. **STEP 7.** (Lower Right) He hand-paints in all of the highlights with opaque acrylics. "This is the secret to making your images really pop." **STEP 8.** (Opposite Page) The final step is to add some color pencil details, "And don't forget to sign your name!"

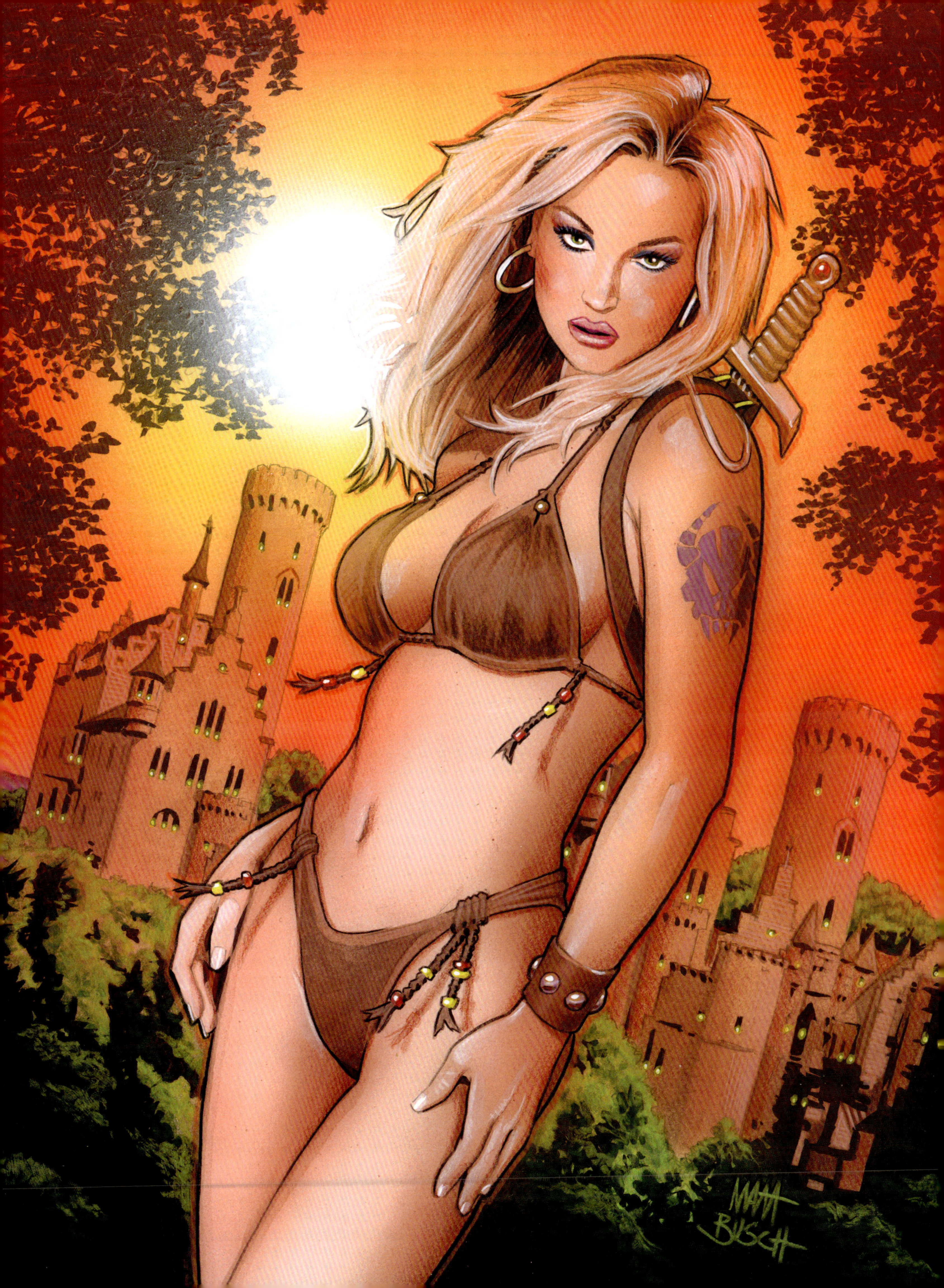
MATT
BUSCH

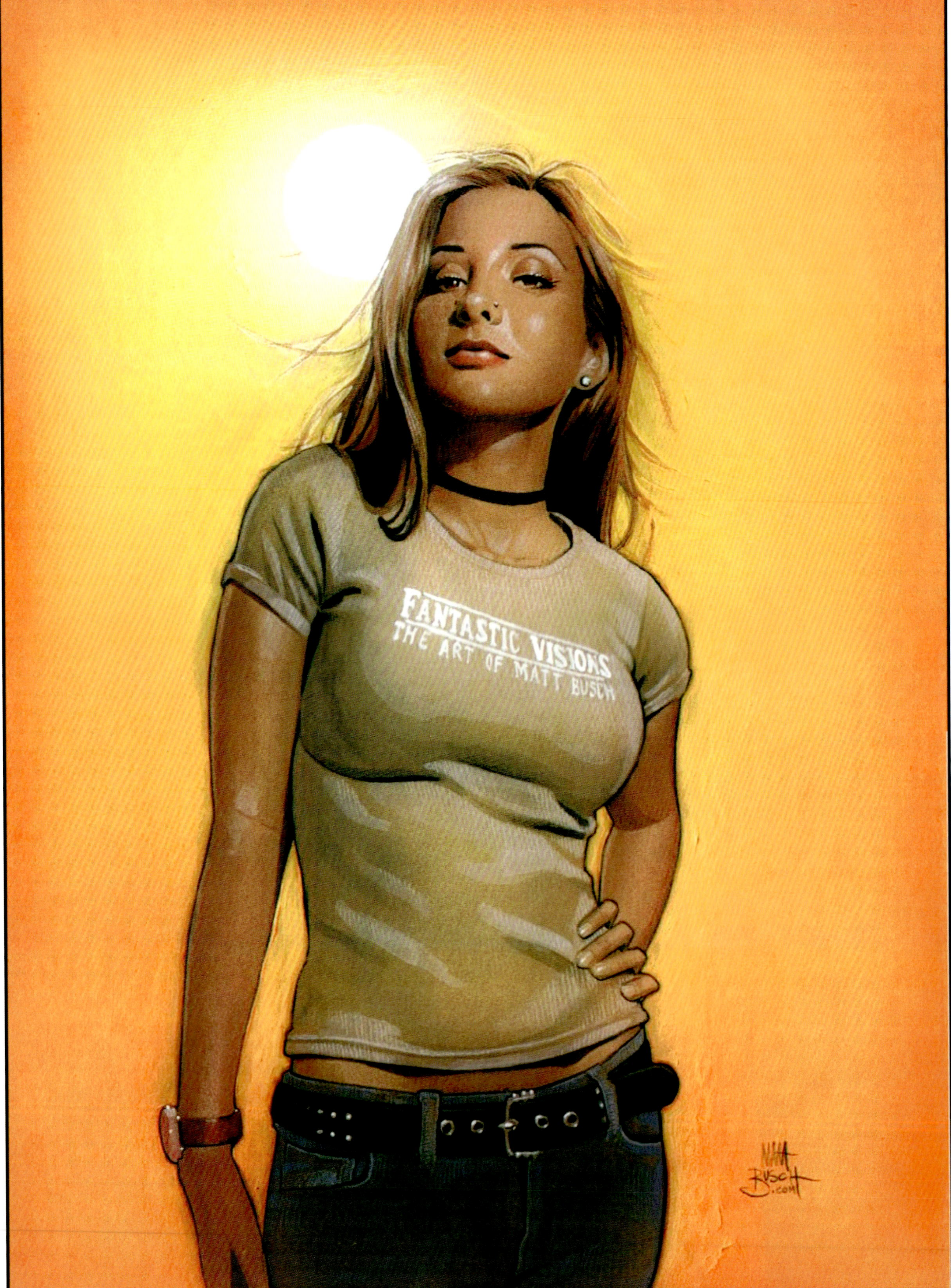
FANTASTIC VISIONS
THE ART OF MATT BUSCH
MATT BUSCH.com

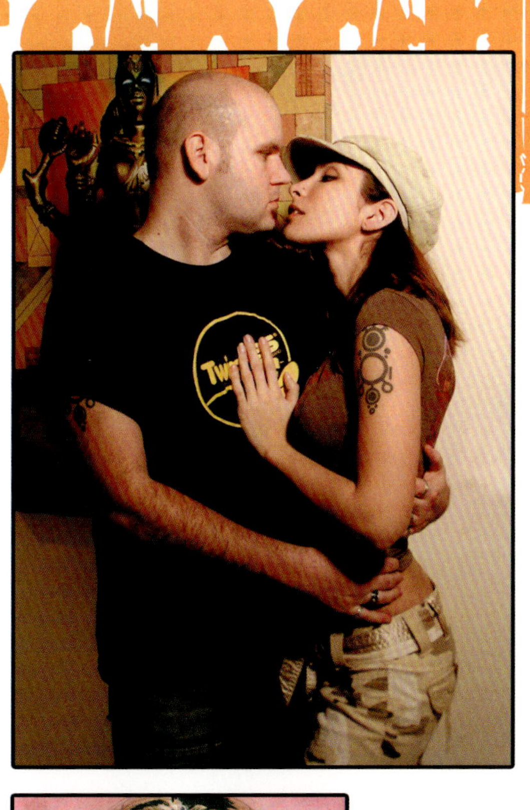

SARAH WILKINSON

In the past, Matt Busch had always kept his work with models professional, and never fell for one of his muses. That changed the day he met Sarah, a young lassie from Oregon who was eager to get into the Entertainment Industry. Busch admits he was smitten with her, but insists that Wilkinson provoked things beyond work. "We hit it off during our first photo-shoot," says Busch, "but when we were done, Sarah seemed like something was troubling her. Out of nowhere, Sarah said, 'It would be wrong for me to kiss you...'" Who would not argue that!

Since dating Busch, Wilkinson's dreams of the spotlight have come true. You can see Sarah in much of Busch's art on projects like TOMB RAIDER, FANTASTIC VISIONS, DETROIT MUSIC AWARDS, The RAIN, FEMME FATALES, SHI, HARMONY for SIRENS OF CINEMA, and tons of merchandise for the band POISON. Sarah has also tried her hand at acting, having co-starred with Busch in his first independent movie, CONJURE. You can find out more, and see additional saucy photos of Sarah at ConjureTheMovie.com.

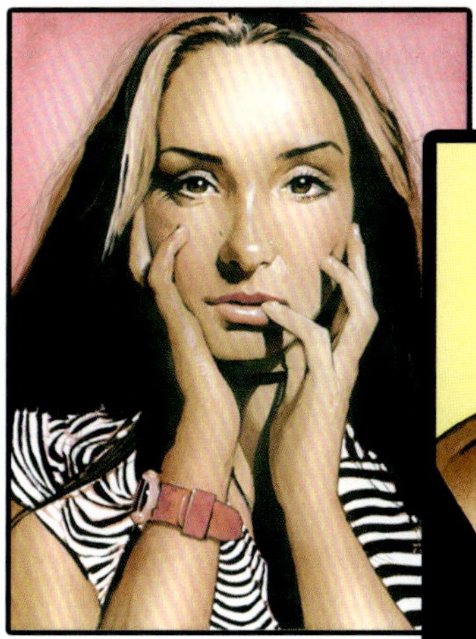

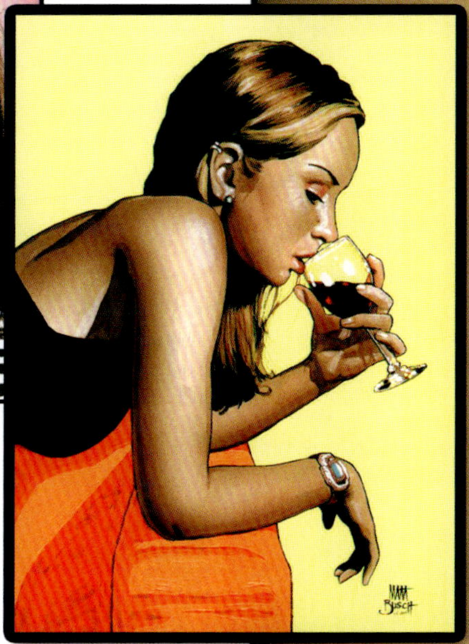

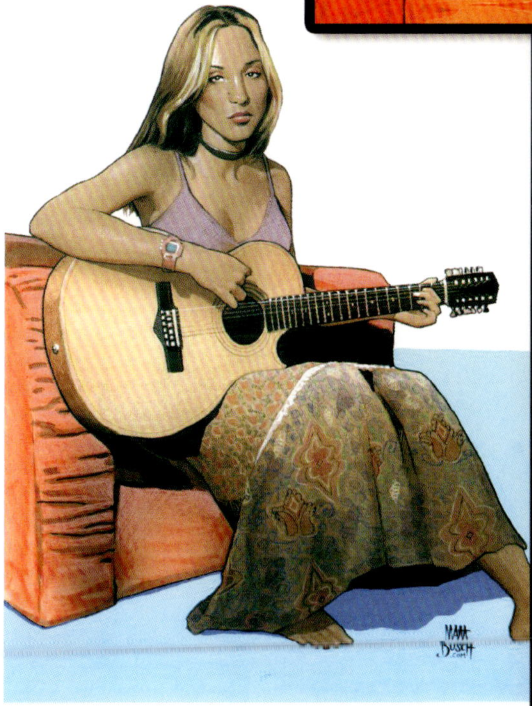

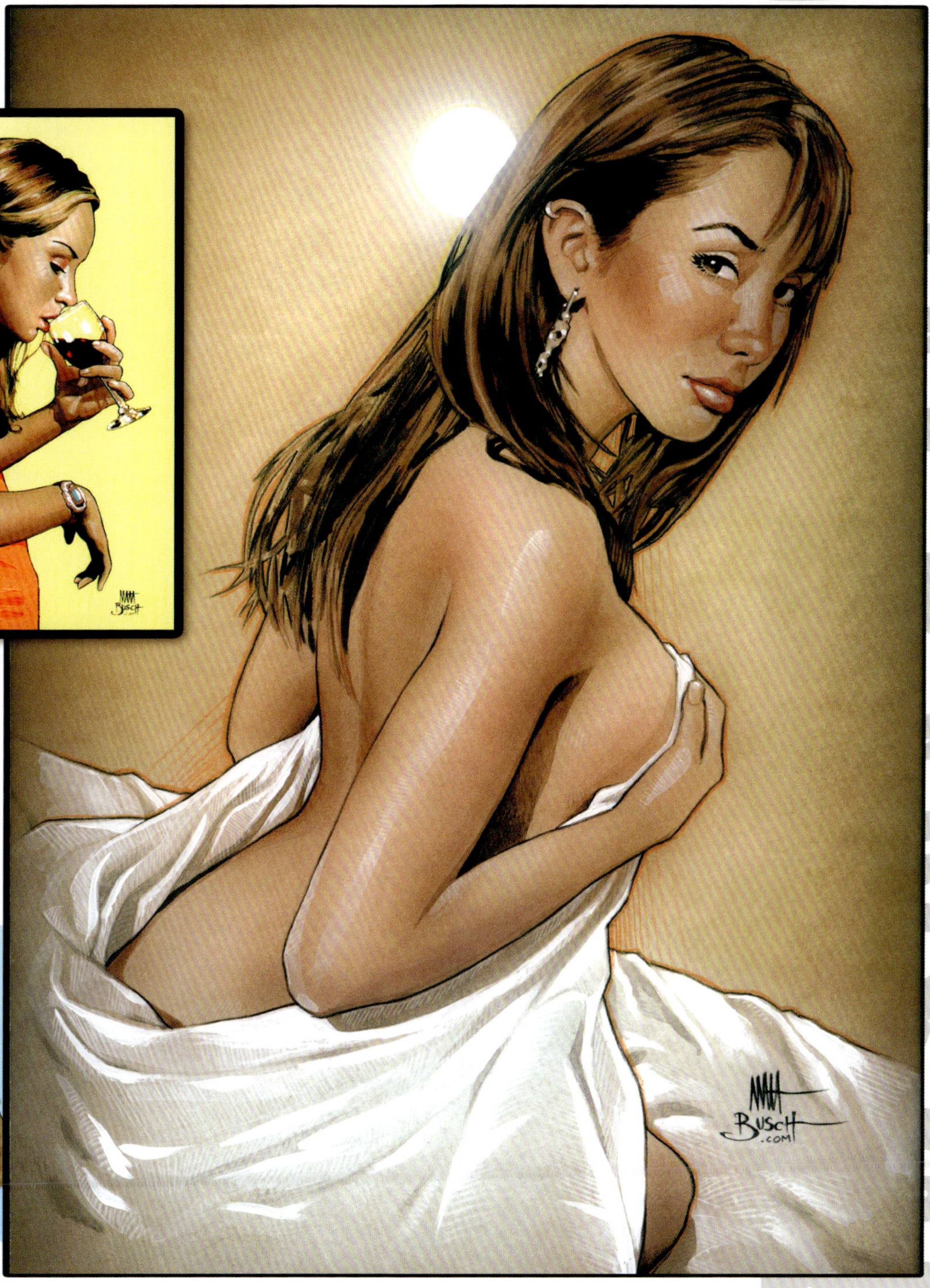

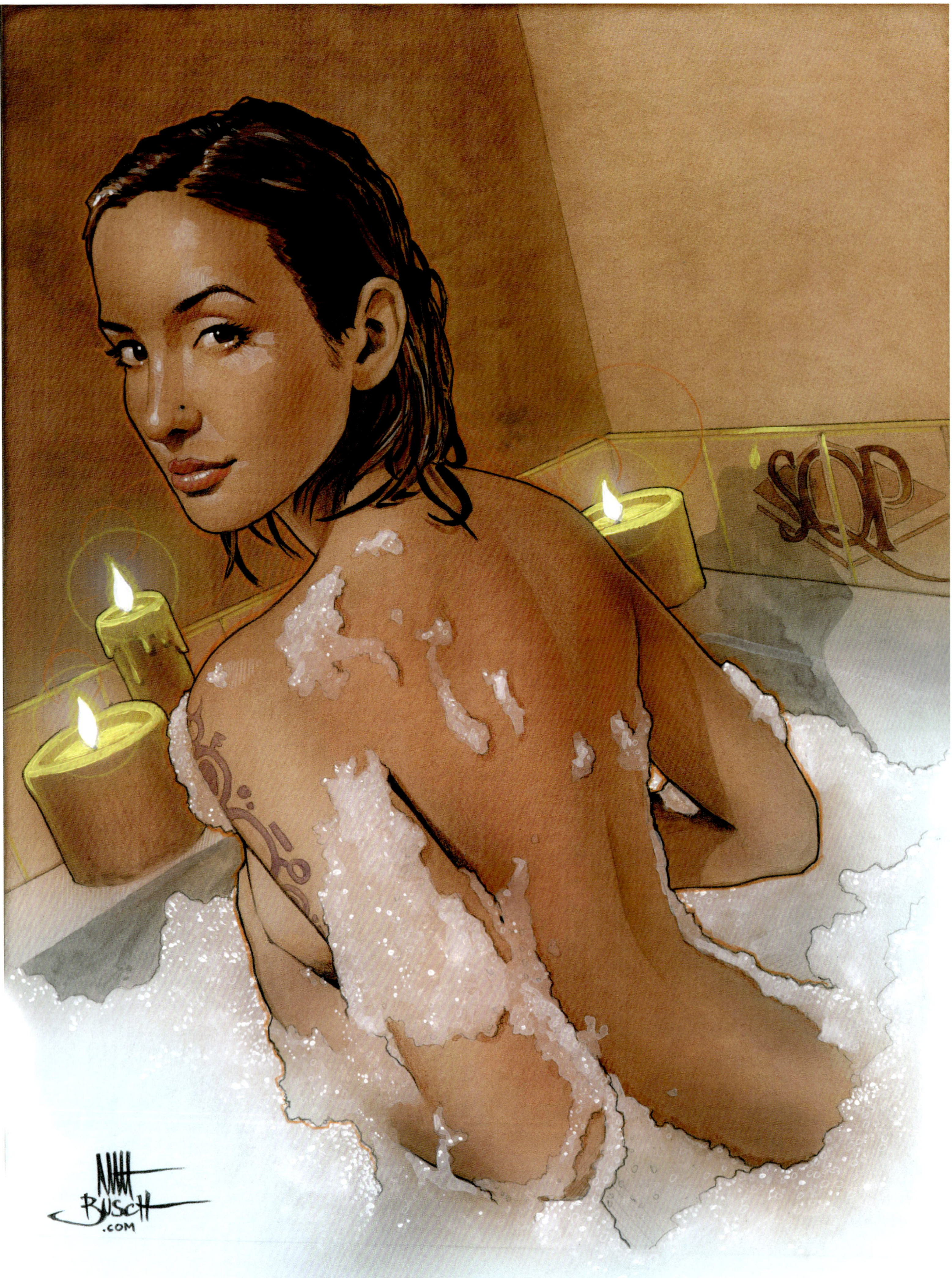
SOP
BUSCH
.COM

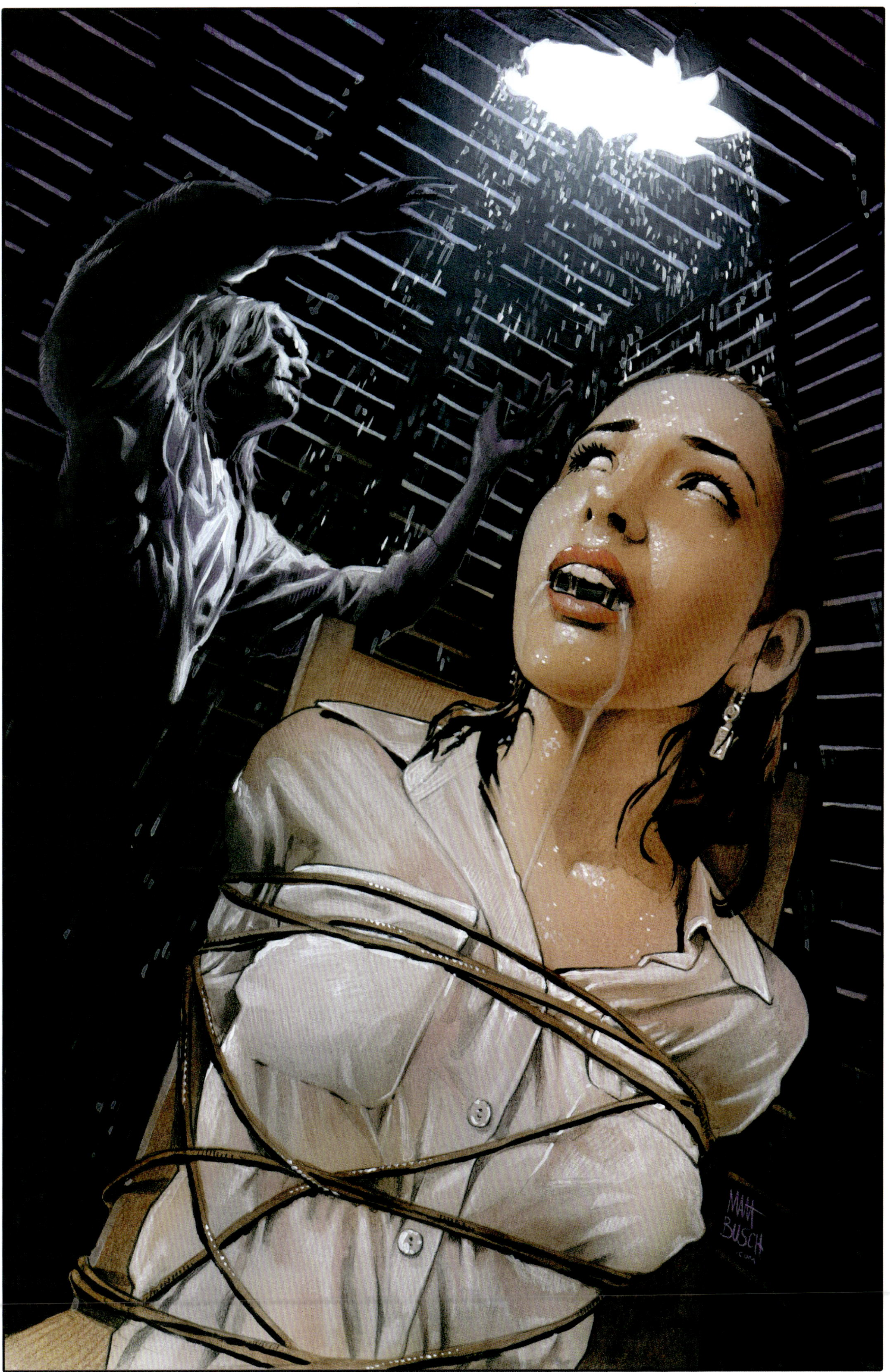
MATT
BUSCH
.com

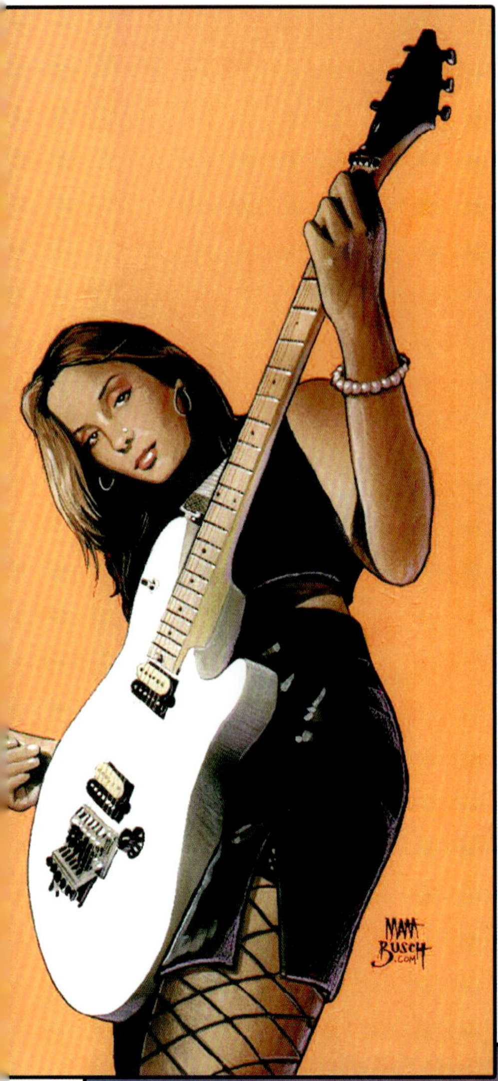

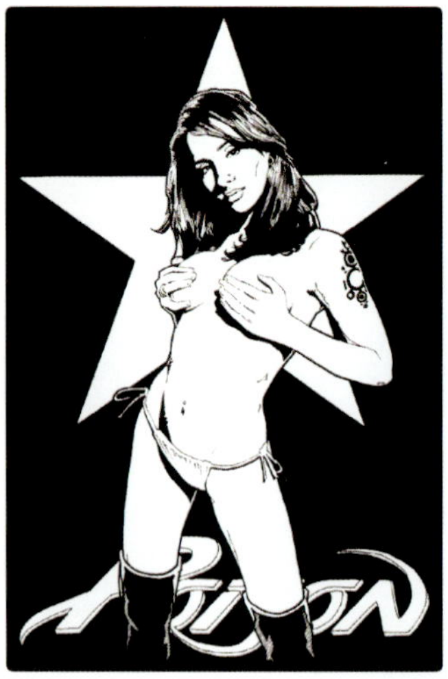

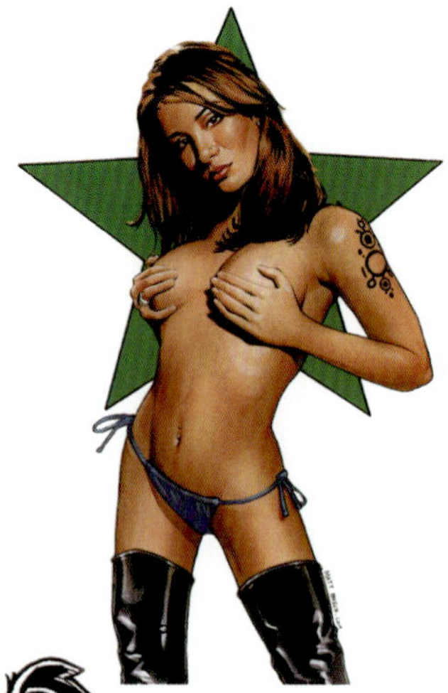

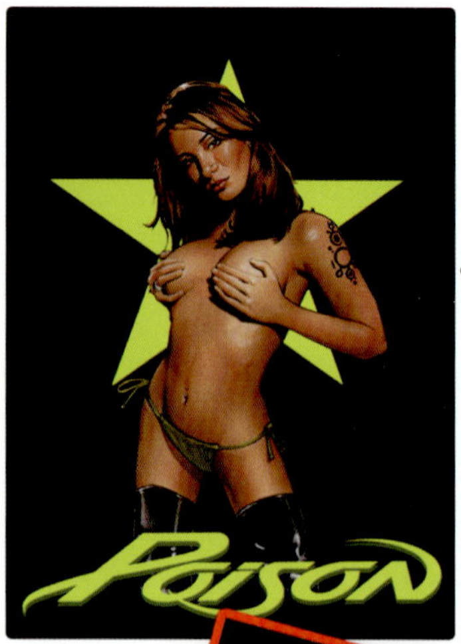

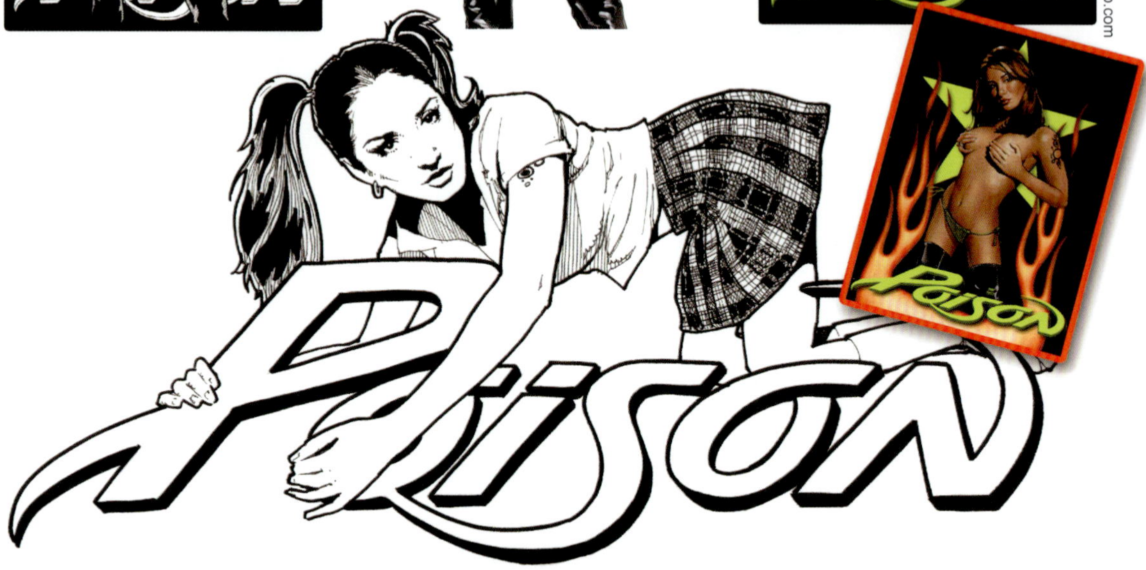

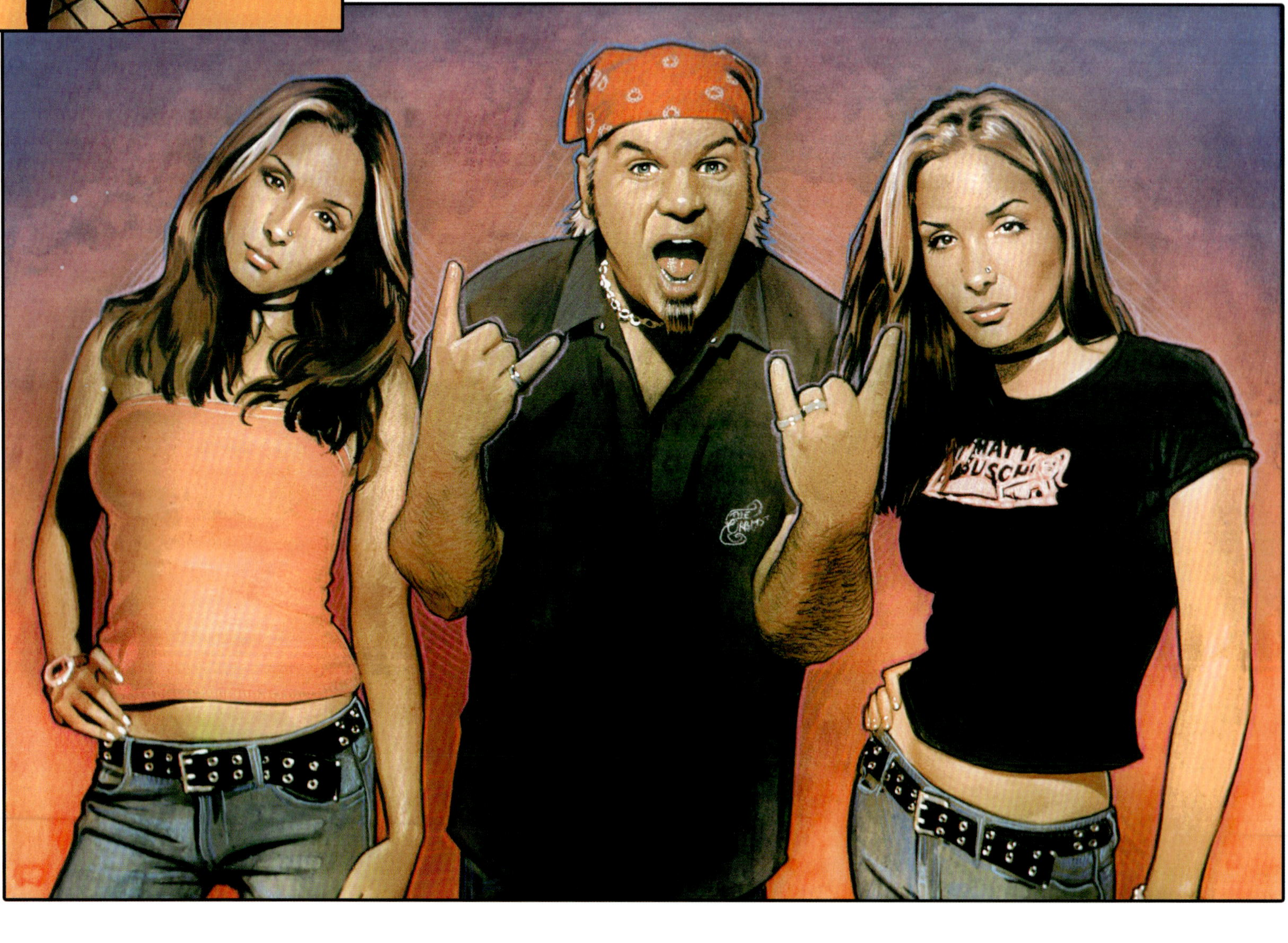

POISON © 2006 SONY Signatures Network. www.PoisonWeb.com

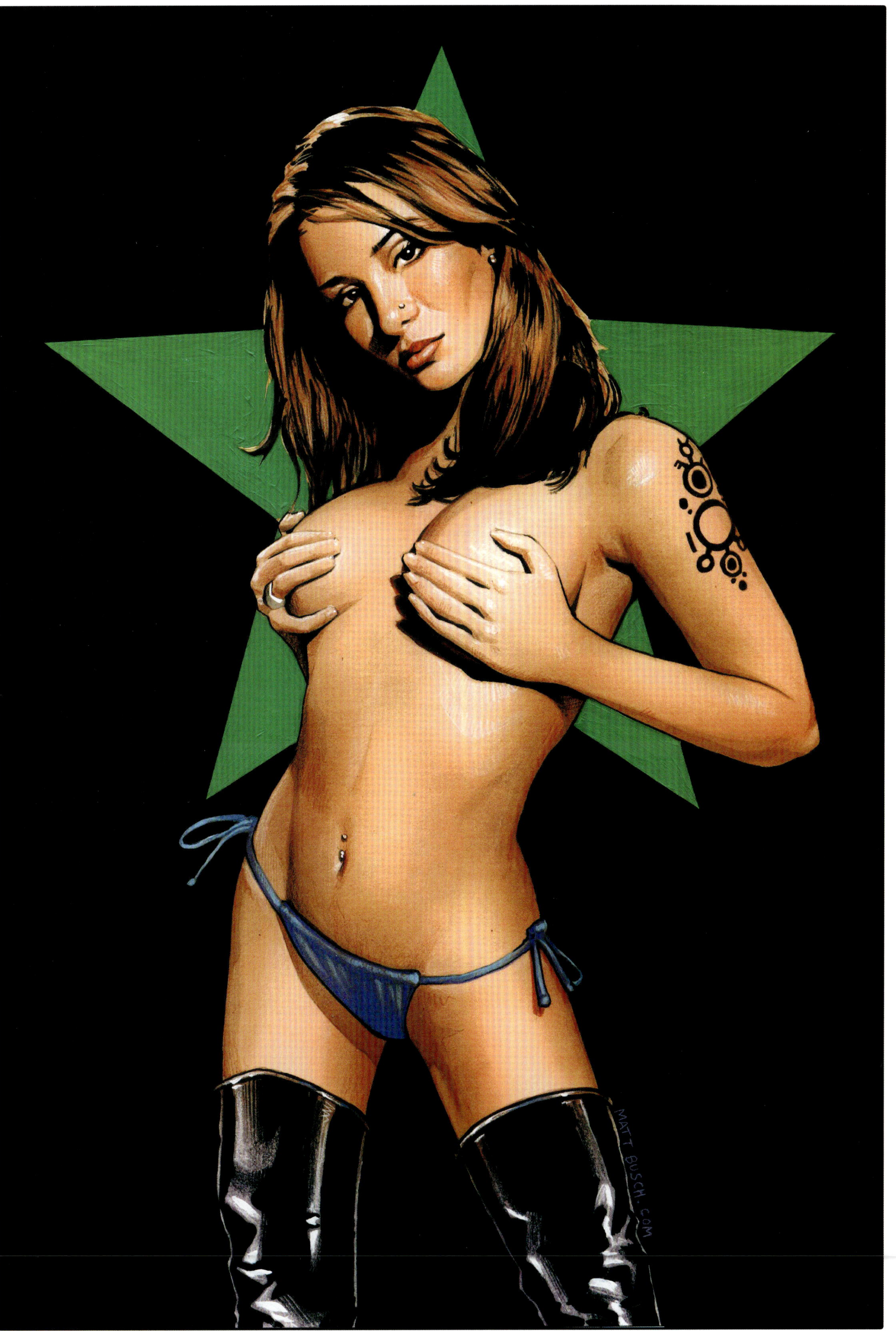
MATT BUSCH.COM

SHI

Over the years, Busch has worked with Billy Tucci on a number of SHI projects. Most recently, Busch took such an opportunity to also work with Sarah Wilkinson creatively in a way he never had before. Sarah had already modeled for Tucci as the Illustrated Warrior, but this time, Busch co-illustrated SHI with Sarah herself. Matt has also helped Sarah to work on such properties as STAR WARS, LORD OF THE RINGS and MY LITTLE PONY.

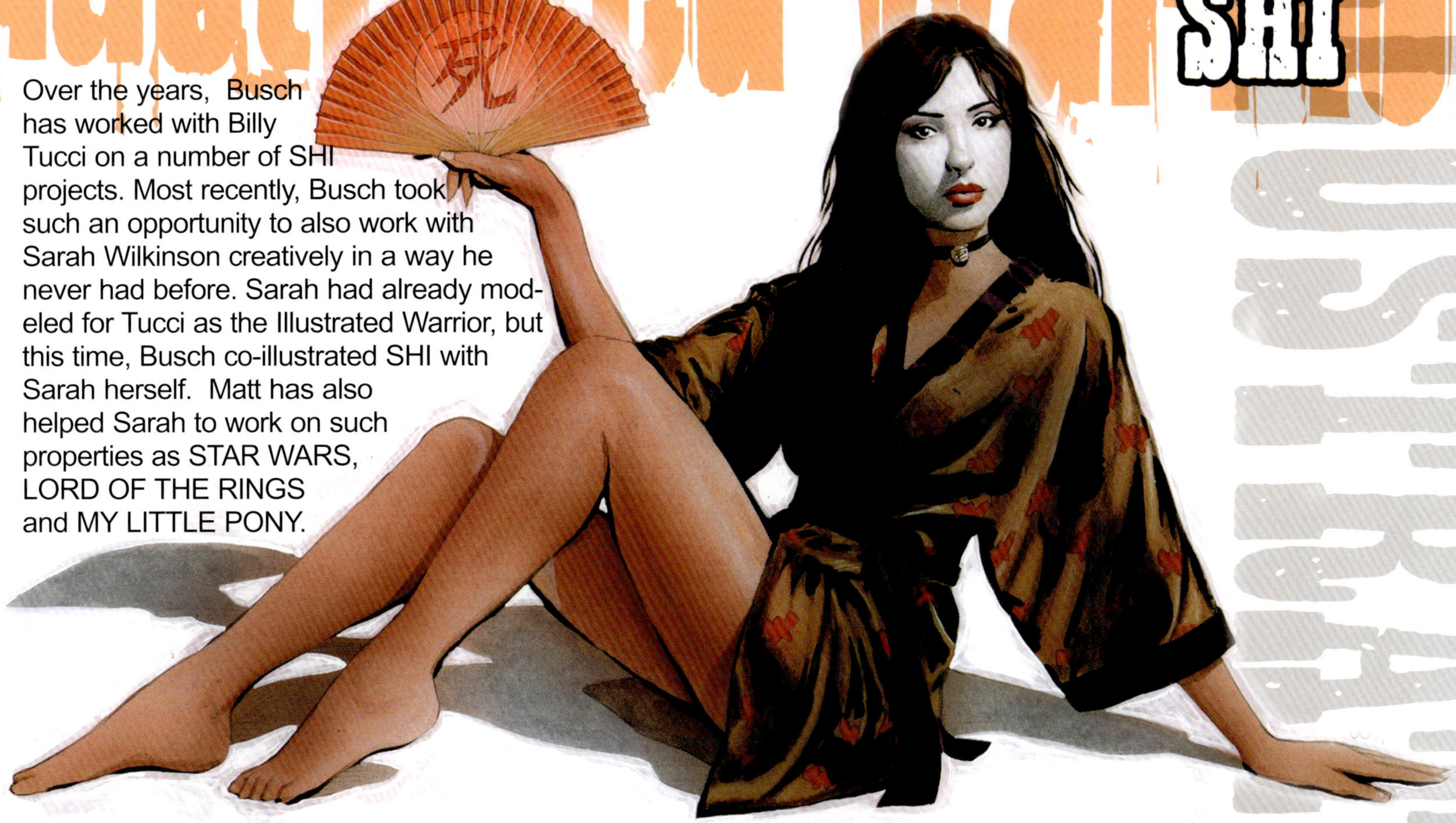

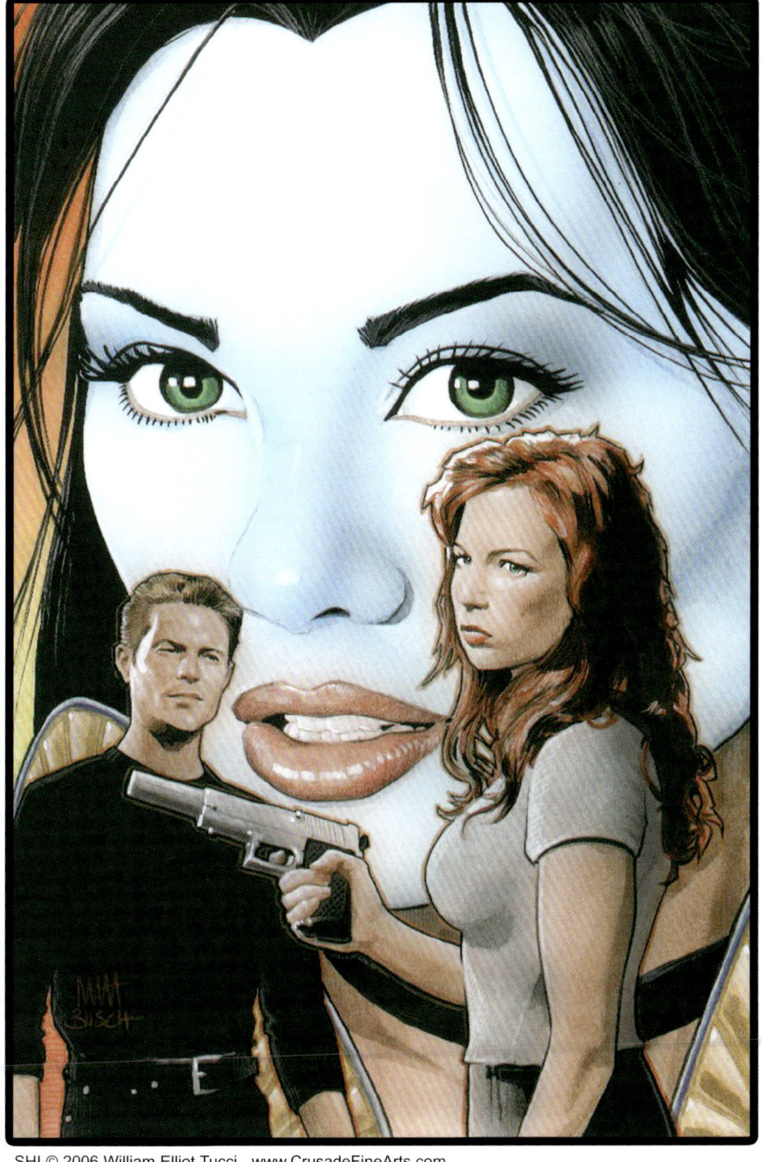

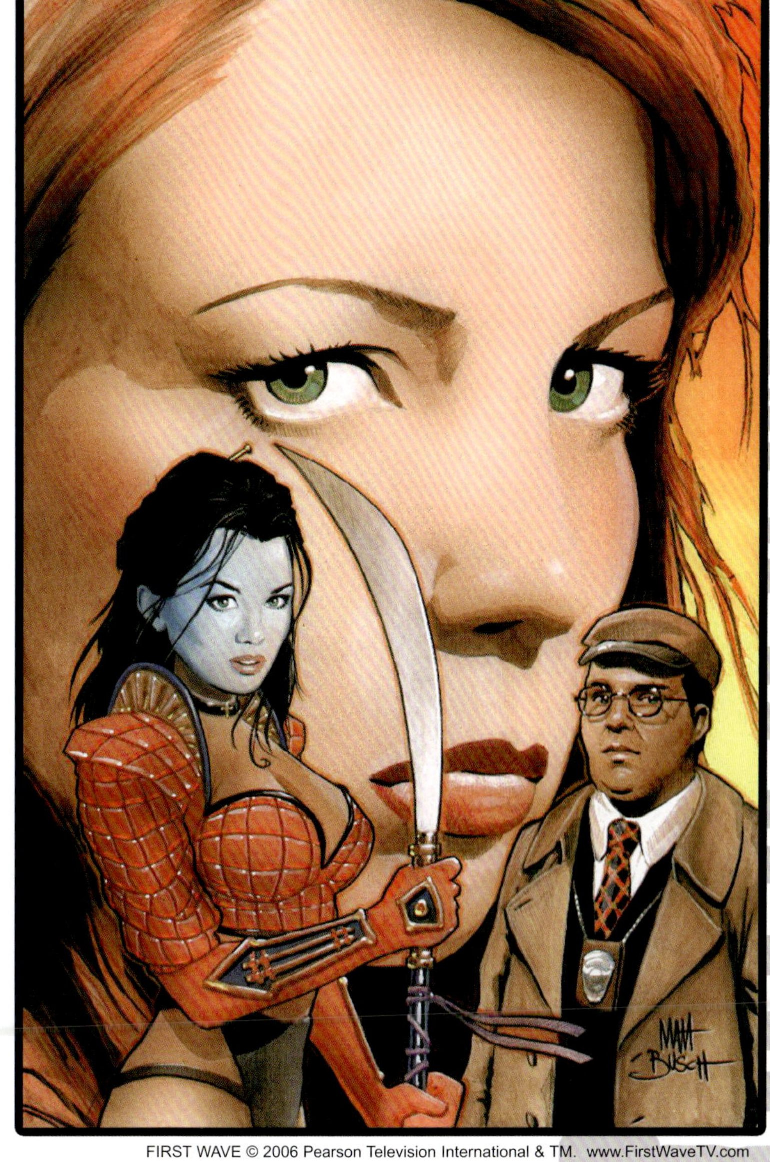

SHI © 2006 William Elliot Tucci. www.CrusadeFineArts.com

FIRST WAVE © 2006 Pearson Television International & TM. www.FirstWaveTV.com

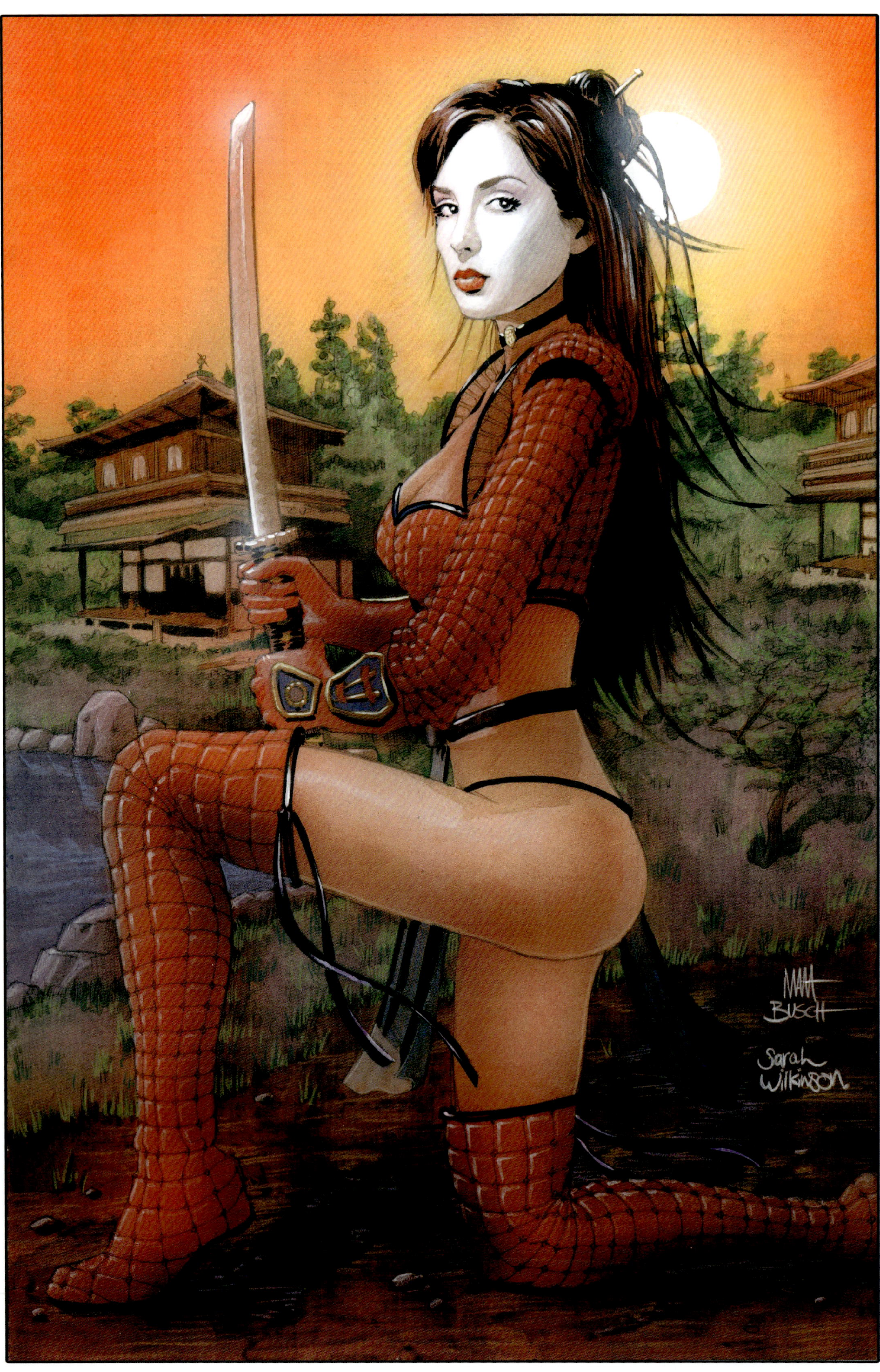
MATT BUSCH
Sarah Wilkinson

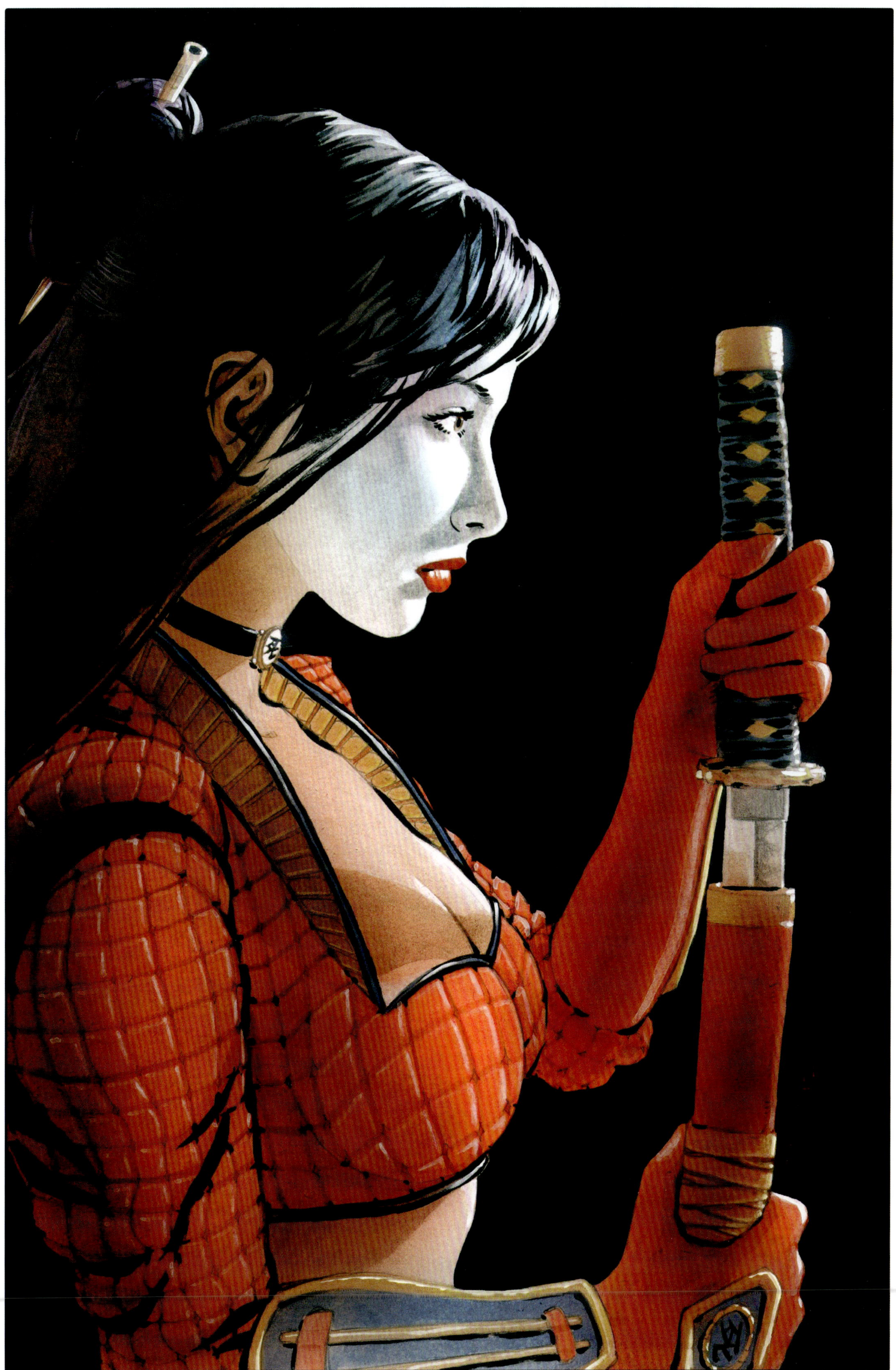

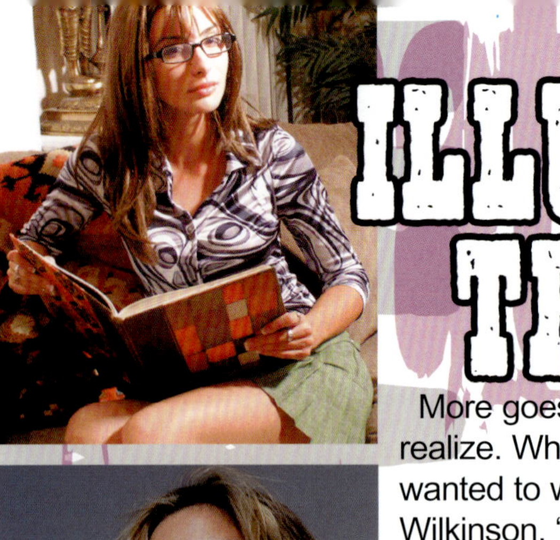

ILLUSTRATING THE COVER

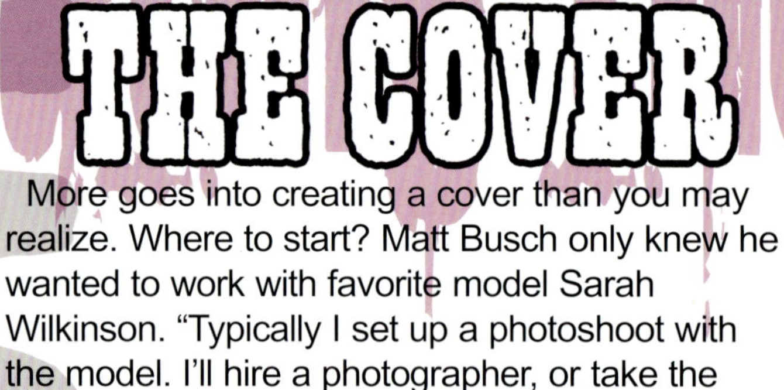

More goes into creating a cover than you may realize. Where to start? Matt Busch only knew he wanted to work with favorite model Sarah Wilkinson. "Typically I set up a photoshoot with the model. I'll hire a photographer, or take the photos myself if I know exactly what I want." These photos of Wilkinson (Left) are shot by Busch, Frank Lombardo and Andy Bloedow.

Next, Busch will often draw up several cover sketches to offer options. "The folks at SQP were involved in helping me choose the best eye-catching cover. In this case, it was great, because the ones not chosen still made it into the book."

Lastly, Busch will often whip up a color comp (Upper Right) as practice. "These studies only take an hour or two, but they help me see where I want to go color-wise, before going on to the final (Opposite Page)."

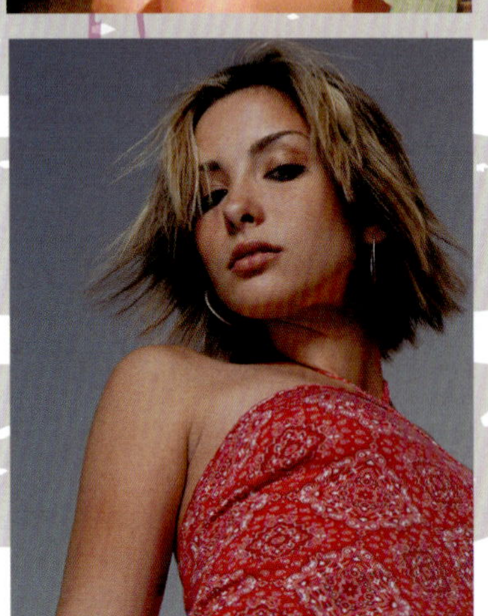

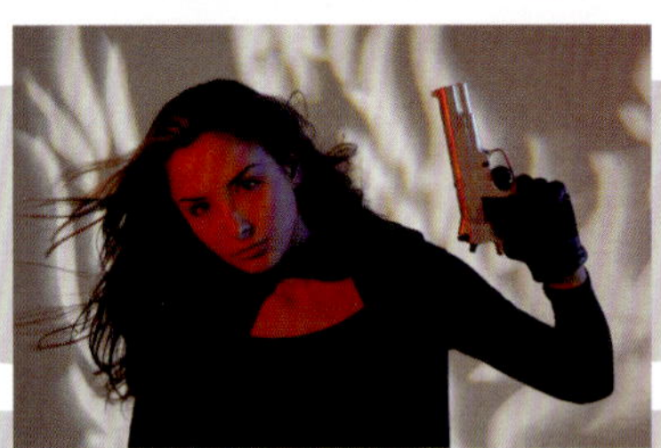

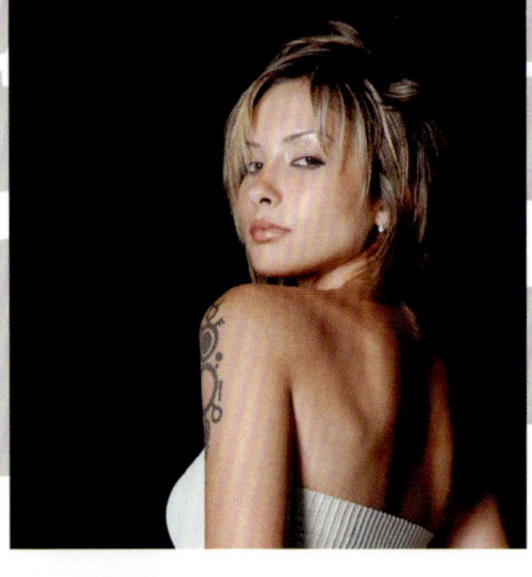

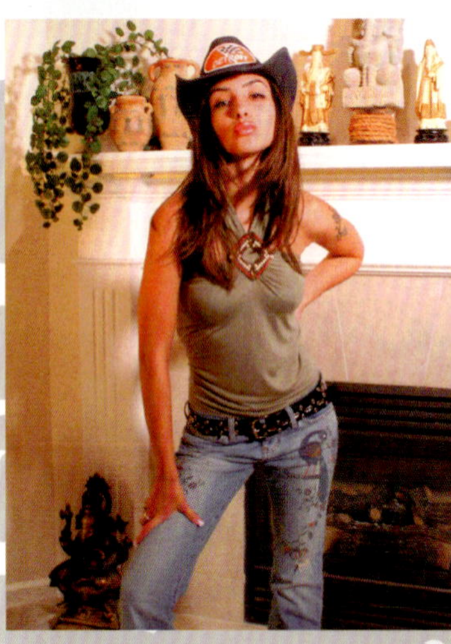

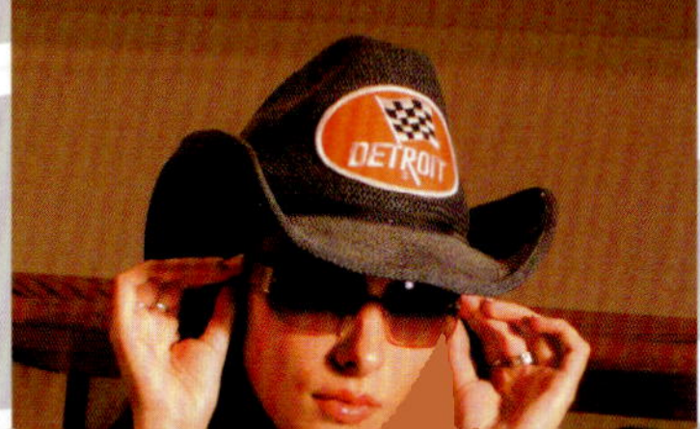

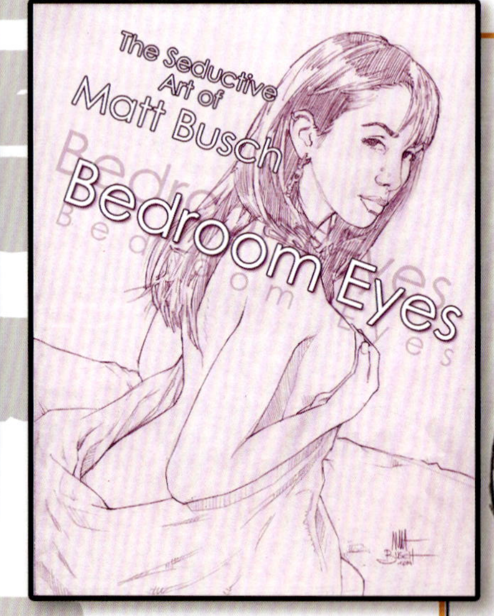

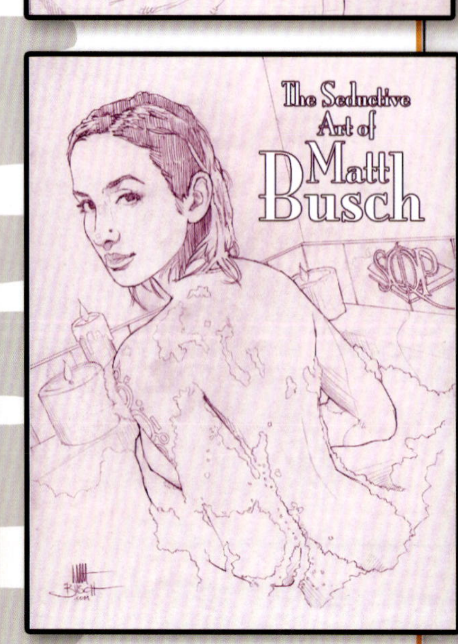

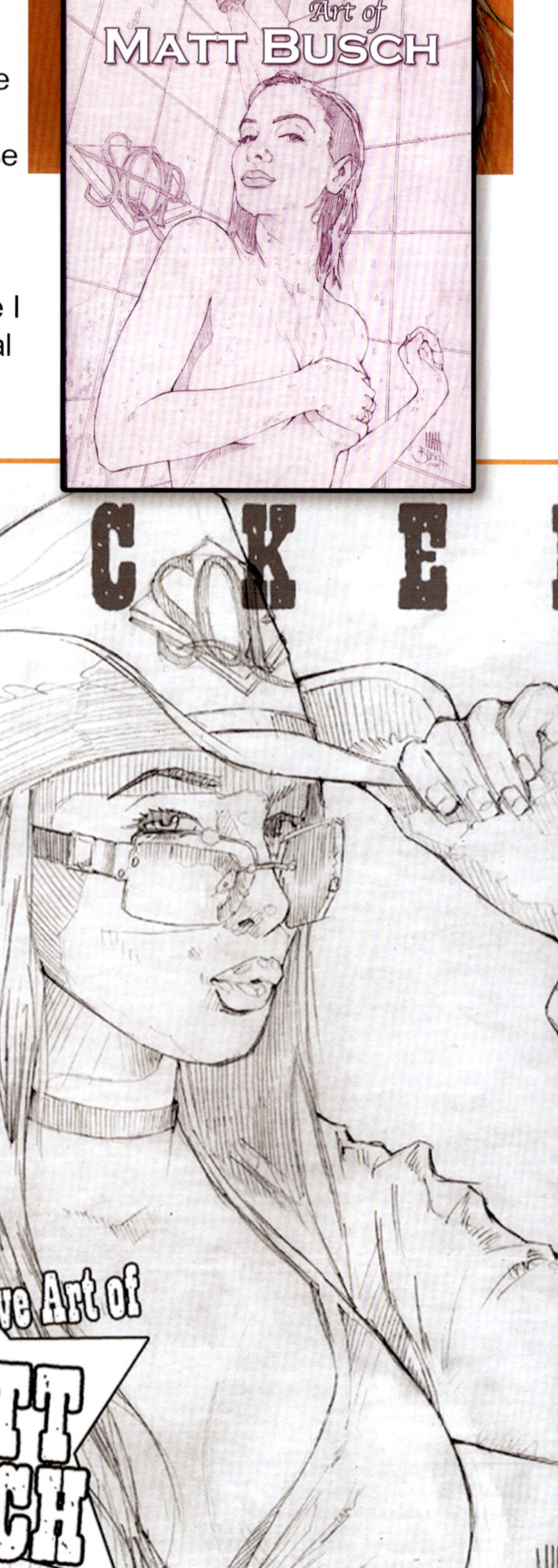

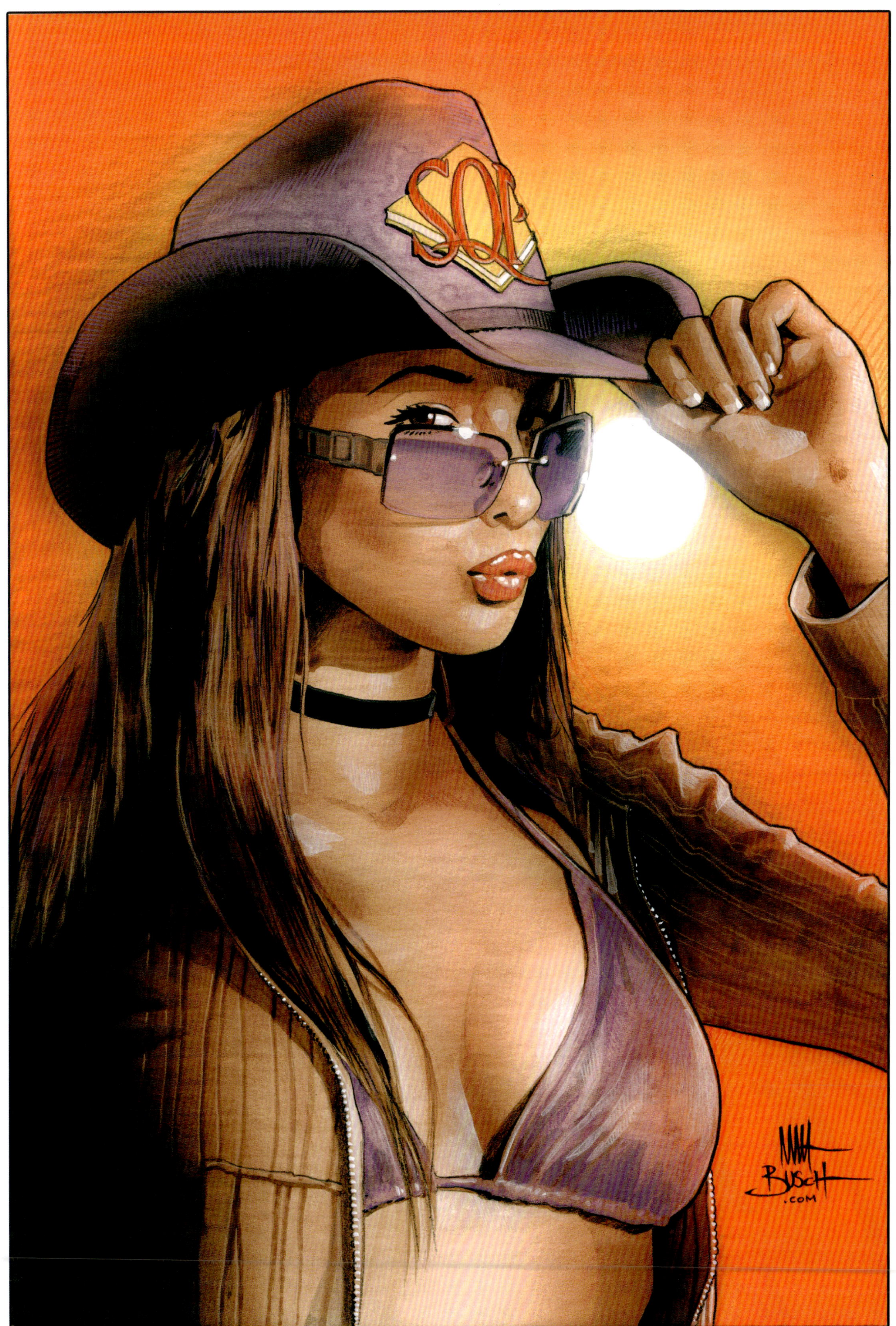
SQP
BUSCH
.com

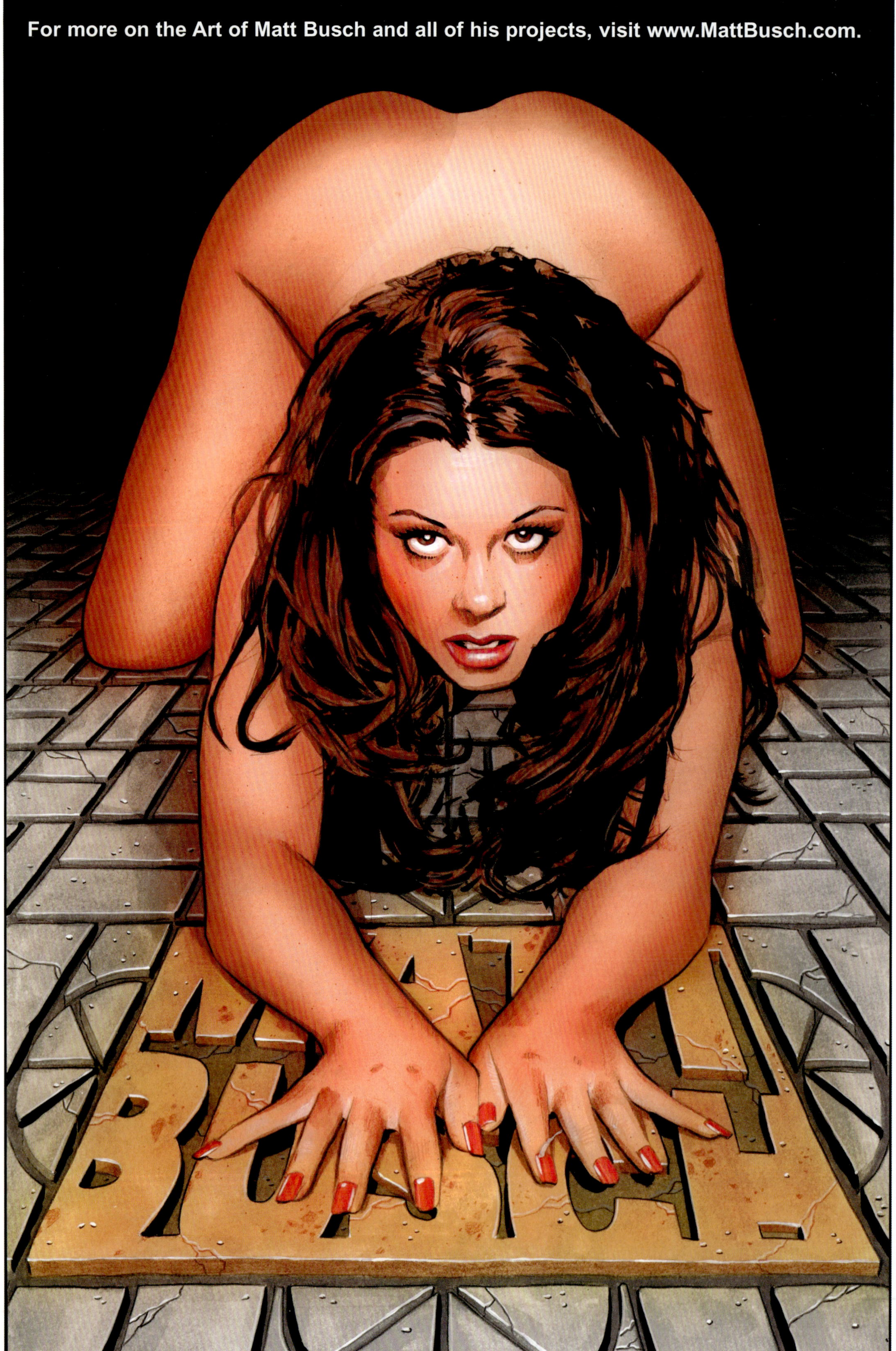

All artwork and characters unless otherwise noted © 2006 PlanetmattEntertainment.

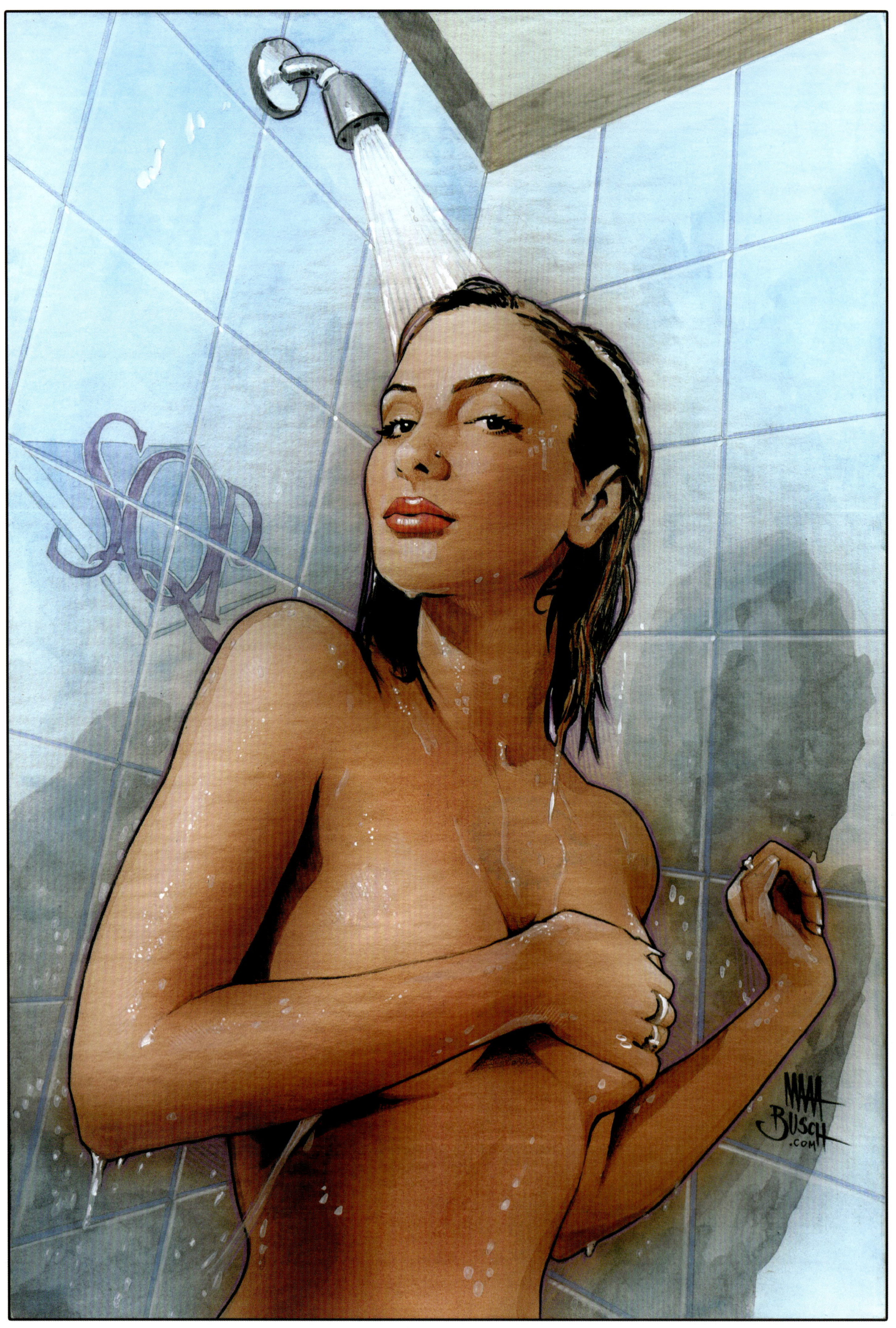
SQP
BUSCH
.COM